Heave To!

You'll Drown Yourselves!

Cover photo: Aerial view of six-square-acre Depoe Bay harbor. Rock-rimmed, fifty-foot-wide channel twists a hundred yards under Coast Highway U.S. 101 bridge to Pacific Ocean. When author first navigated channel in 1938, it was only twenty feet wide and, along with the harbor, was not navigable at less than half tide. (From author's collection)

Twenty-eight-foot former gillnetter *Tradewinds* being navigated through Depoe Bay channel by the author following deep-sea fishing trip in 1938. Rock-rimmed channel, squeezed down to twenty-foot width at that time, was widened to fifty feet in 1966. (From author's collection)

Heave To!
You'll Drown Yourselves!

Stan Allyn

Binford & Mort Publishing
2536 S.E. Eleventh • Portland, Oregon 97202

Dedication

To my late wife, Elsie

PREFACE

By a mariner's miracle a swell shoved the conked-out craft through the twisting, rock-rimmed channel into the tiny harbor, where Allyn made repairs and started the charter-fishing business he still owns and operates with his son Richard.

This true tale centers around his first turbulent year in charter fishing and relates hairbreadth escapes from disaster, storms, shipwrecks, drownings, murder, rum runners, evidence of cannibalism on a derelict Japanese fishing vessel, sharks, whales, strange sea creatures, the Japanese Current and its bounty, tsunami tidal waves, giant wind waves and other sea experiences, sparked with salty language, humor and lively style.

Spliced into it are some history of Depoe Bay and the area, bits of sea-sense advice to beginning mariners and hints on catching Pacific Salmon.

S.A.

CONTENTS

Russian merchant ship *Vazlaz Vorovsky*, pounded by breakers to total loss in April, 1941, off inner end of north Columbia River jetty near spot where Coast Guard bosun's mate aboard motor lifeboat averted near-certain disaster to the author and his vessel in May, 1938, when he ordered "heave to." (Photo by Larry Barber)

1. Broached

The distant thunder of breakers on the Columbia River bar boomed warning of violent death to unheeding mariners.

My landlubber brain didn't spark. Braced against the wheelhouse bulkhead, I continued steering my twenty-eight-foot converted gillnetter seaward down the lower Columbia River channel into steepening ocean-spawned swells.

The spectacle of heavy breakers rampaging across Desdemona Sands—a nearby channel-edge sandspit, six miles upriver from the bar—should have shot reminders to my two crewmen and me of the disaster that gave the spit its name. It was on New Year's Day in 1857 that the deeply laden bark, *Desdemona*, labored inbound across the bar through heavy swells, then smashed to destruction on this breaker-bashed, sandy river shoal.

Breakers ahead on the bar were a near cinch to add us to the death log of hundreds of vessels and mariners dashed to oblivion there since adventurous young Yankee explorer, Captain Robert Gray, logged his notch in history by sailing the *Columbia Rediviva* between breakers and shoals into the then-unexplored river, May 11, 1792.

But warnings thrust by danger signs and past disasters dimmed in our minds like a lighthouse in the fog. The two big cylinders of our 1914-vintage, eight-horsepower Frisco Standard marine engine were rattle-banging the gillnetter through the mounting seas at a solid six knots.

We were getting a charge out of roller-coastering over the swells in our first taste of saltwater sailing. Nor did we take heed of another insidious warning—the absence of other

1

vessels on this normally heavily trafficked great river, swirling its million cubic feet per second of Canadian Rockies-born water toward head-on collision with inrushing Pacific seas.

We thrashed on—three dumb young landlubbers in our early twenties, blundering toward disaster on this overcast spring day in 1938. Two years before, I'd plunked out $350 to buy the aging gillnetter at Portland, Oregon, the city of my birth and my habitat until now.

On days off from my job at the old Portland *News Telegram*, I remodeled and enlarged the craft's tiny cabin and pleasure-cruised it on the placid, protected waters of the Willamette and Columbia rivers near Portland.

During those two years, brain waves that started as a whisper grew to a shout. I finally decided to scuttle the newspaper job and challenge the Pacific in a deep-sea fishing venture.

As I sanded, painted, rigged and readied the little double-ender, round-bottomed craft in the quiet water alongside the Portland dock, my thoughts sheered away from the newspaper and the city and drowsed through ideas for a good name. . . . *Tradewinds!* She would sail and fish as steady as the trade winds blow.

By the time I'd lettered *Tradewinds* in bold, black letters on both flared bows, I'd convinced myself that *Tradewinds* and I were going to conquer the Pacific. My family and friends did not share my enthusiasm.

"Crazy as a landlocked loon," they wailed. "You'll drown yourself."

Their expostulations bounced off my brain like sea water off a gull's back. I threw myself into my sea preparations with renewed vigor.

Just after midnight on an overcast night in May 1938, two landlubber friends and I finished stowing gear and chow aboard. I primed the cylinders, treadmilled the big flywheel into fast spin, and kicked in the compression levers. The Frisco Standard ka-chuck, ka-chucked into stentorian action, drowning out the farewell dirge of hand-wringing family and friends.

We cast off and were underway down the dark, freshet-swollen Columbia.

Twenty-eight-foot Columbia River gillnetter after it was remodeled, sail-rigged, and christened *Tradewinds* by the author in 1937. Photo was taken by author while vessel was anchored in front of Multnomah Falls during shakedown cruise.

Ahead of us lay a 205-mile haul—105 miles down the Columbia to the Pacific Ocean; then south along the rugged Oregon coast a hundred miles to tiny, rock-rimmed Depoe Bay, from where we'd show the world how to operate a deep-sea fishing business.

Could I have foreseen that storm, shipwreck, murder and death would beset my course through the turbulent sea miles ahead, I'd probably have shut off the Frisco Standard on the spot and highballed back to the city.

Like most small vessels in the 1930s, we did not have radio, radar, depth sounder or any other electronic gear. Two cylinders, sails I'd rigged as a back-up in case the Frisco Standard conked, and one magnetic compass comprised our total equipment.

We'd churned the hundred miles from Portland to Desdemona Sands without serious incident, and now, with no electronic means of getting a Coast Guard bar or weather report, we chugged blindly along into steepening seas whose racing crests were starting to curl and snarl with increasing force.

So intently were we peering ahead through the spray-splashed windshield, we failed to spot a white speck astern that grew to a thirty-six-foot Coast Guard motor lifeboat frothing toward us.

A slicker-clad coastguardsman in the plunging craft's forward cockpit was alternately ducking spray and windmilling his arms at us. The lifeboat clawed to a couple of fathoms off our starboard beam.

At the helm, a burly bosun's mate, his anger-reddened face scowling the demons of the deep at us, bellowed through cupped hands, "Heave to! You'll drown yourselves!"

I chopped the throttle—not a whale's whisker too soon. The gillnetter heaved skyward up the face of a towering green sea, plunged through its curling crest, then plummeted to the following trough with a bonejarring whop that drove us to our knees.

Grabbing the helm, I hauled myself upright and had just started to muscle the helm to port when the next hissing crest slammed us broadside, hammered us onto beam's end; and the gillnetter shot down the wave's roiling face on its side.

Depoe Bay Coast Guard 36-foot motor lifeboat slamming into towering breaker, while out-bound through Depoe Bay channel on assistance mission.

Bosun's mate aboard a similar motor lifeboat probably saved the lives of author Allyn and his companions when he hauled alongside author's converted Columbia River gillnetter *Tradewinds*, heading outbound toward murderous Columbia River bar, and bellowed: "Heave to! You'll drown yourselves!" (Photo by author)

I rammed the gear lever astern, backed full, and by sheer dumb luck got the embattled bucket's beam's-end skid stopped, then wrenched her around to port. She righted herself, headed upriver.

Now running with the seas, *Tradewinds* easily slid down their steep faces, vibrated to a stop as the following troughs nearly swallowed her—then hurtled ahead on the next crest, gradually gaining headway toward safe water.

The motor lifeboat, with sea water belching from her scuppers, had also got squared around and was thrashing a parallel upriver course off our port quarter. When we reached safe water above Desdemona Sands, the bosun's mate hailed us to haul to the Point Adams Coast Guard Station on the Oregon shore. We hauled and moored.

Two coastguardsmen inspected *Tradewinds* and its equipment, while the bosun's mate wrote things on a form. This done, with deceptively elaborate calm he fished a cigarette from a crumpled pack, thumbnailed a match alight, lit off, inhaled deeply, and confronted me.

"Might I ask, sir," he breathed with exaggerated politeness, "what you were doing heading out on that bar when it's so G--**##!!*# rough it's closed to all shipping!"

"Seemed all right to us," I quavered. "We thought it was always like that."

A blast of cigarette smoke exploded from his mouth. As if performing a pagan rite, he raised clenched fists to face level, rolled his eyes heavenward, and called upon all the gods of all the skies and all the seas to please deliver him from future dealings with such bilge-brained lubbers as us.

"Now get that bucket outta here—thataway!" he roared, jerking his thumb upriver. We got underway—thataway.

A fine spray grew to a whirling deluge of bilge water, flung throughout the engine compartment by the big flywheel. The buffeting on the bar had loosened calking, which outside pressure had now torn loose, letting the Columbia River gurgle into the hull.

The Frisco Standard started to hiccup and burp. The bilge bath was drowning the ignition. We yanked up the bilge boards and rammed in the suction end of our only pump—a big, portable hand-operated job. The damn thing didn't even start breathing hard, let alone suck.

We were a cinch for the deep-six if we didn't do something—quick!

We emptied our coffee pot over the side, followed it with the contents of a two-pound coffee can, and used the pot and can to bail for our lives. The dripping Frisco Standard was gasping on one lung now. The flooding bilge was steadily winning the bail battle.

On our starboard yawned the entrance to Youngs Bay, flanking the west side of Astoria, twelve miles upriver from the bar. We swung to starboard and bailed and chugged a precarious mile or so up the bay to where a tidal mud flat showed on the east shore.

Mud never looked so good. We helmed to port, struggled toward the mud flat, then squooshed to a stop in a quagmire of goo covered with a couple of feet of water.

While my crewmen cleared our two anchors for dropping fore and aft, I untied the lines from a skiff I'd lashed to the foredeck before leaving Portland.

Struggling to launch the skiff so we could get ashore, I managed the remarkable feat of heaving myself into the drink instead of the skiff—stern first with a mighty, muddy splash.

My deep-sea career was launched—literally!

2. Conked

Scouting the area the next day, we found a small stretch of solid, sandy beach. We worked *Tradewinds* onto it, careened her and spent several days stripping out old calking and pounding in new.

While we were banging away with hammers and calking irons, an old weather-etched commercial fisherman, who'd heard of our bar battle, sauntered alongside, knocked the ashes from a battered corncob, and offered sea-sense advice.

"Always get a bar and weather report before heading to sea," he cautioned, refilling the corncob. "And never cross the bar on the ebb. A bar that's safe during flood tide when the incoming seas and tide are running in the same direction can become a killer on the ebb when the outrushing tide and river current bust head-on into incoming seas."

He held a match above the corncob, sucked for several seconds, then went on, "Make sure your compass is working right and has been compensated for deviation. Metal objects aboard can pull the compass out of alignment. During poor visibility that can make the difference between safety and shipwreck.

"Install a barometer in the wheelhouse where you can watch it. Steady around thirty is usually a fair-weather reading, but if it starts down and keeps dropping—watch out! You're almost for sure in for a blister of a blow from a southerly sector. If it shoots up too far above thirty, you can pretty well figger it's gonna blast from a northerly or easterly direction.

"That bilge pump looks like it came around the Horn with Cap'n Gray on his exploration voyage," he chided. "Get a good one and test it now and then to make sure it works. Keep a good anchor aboard and a spare. Secure ten or so fathoms of chain to the 'ready-for-use' anchor, with forty or more fathoms of stout line secured to the chain; coiled and ready for quick use.

"Make damn sure the bitter end of the anchor line is made fast to the bow bitt or some other solid object before you heave the anchor overboard," he concluded. "Many a mariner fighting to save his craft from reefs, shoals and lee shores has been hurled to destruction because he chucked the anchor overboard and too late watched the unsecured bitter end snake over the side."

A week after our first blundering, bar-crossing attempt, we completed calking, outfitting and readying for sea. We then backed off the beach to a nearby dock and got a telephoned Coast Guard "safe bar and weather report." A brisk east wind had scrubbed the sky clear and knocked down the Pacific's big bar-battering westerly swells.

We chugged from glass-calm Youngs Bay at nine in the evening, allowing plenty of time to cross the bar at close to slack flood, when it was safest; snorted into the Columbia River and headed down-channel under stars that dimmed as a full silver-white moon rose over the jagged Coast Range Mountains to the east. Red, green, and white buoy and beacon lights glimmered and flashed ahead, leading us down the Columbia River channel.

The mariner's three Rs helped: Red Right Returning. When returning from sea, keep red buoys right; thus, when heading to sea, keep red buoys left, black buoys right. Other red, green, and white lights, between the buoys and beacons, we identified as the running lights of approaching vessels.

Here, too, a sailor's memory hook helped. Port wine is red. Red running lights are on a vessel's port side; therefore green lights are on starboard. When vessels are approaching bow-on, pass port to port. We port-to-ported past several vessels and churned between the jetties toward the bar, the moon's luminous glow painting silver lace along the flanking wave-slapped jetty rocks and the gentle sea crests ahead.

So calm was the bar we could scarcely believe that it was

Columbia River Lightship rode on station off the Columbia River entrance when the author took departure south from it for Depoe Bay on his first sea voyage in May, 1938. (Photo by author)

Tillamook Lighthouse's powerful beacon enabled the author to determine his position off the northern Oregon coast when caught in a severe storm in October, 1938. (Photo by author)

the same devil's cauldron that had nearly done us in a week before.

Nor could we envision the hell's broth it must have been two years earlier when its gale-blasted combers sledgehammered the six-thousand-ton freighter *Iowa* from the bar channel and hurled it a half mile north to violent destruction on Peacock Spit's notorious death trap, with the loss of all thirty-four hands.

Clear of the jetty heads, we rollicked six miles over long, gentle ground swells on a southwesterly course to the bright-red-hulled Columbia River Lightship, beaming its six-hundred-thousand-candlepower beacon into the night. At the gently rolling lightship we swung to a southerly heading for the hundred-mile haul to Depoe Bay, using yet another mariner's jingle to plot our correct course: If variation is west, compass course is best; if variation is east, compass course is least.

We subtracted the twenty-one degrees easterly variation shown on the chart for this portion of the ocean and chugged south through the moon-washed night on a course parallel to the rugged, Coast Range-flanked Oregon coast.

Tradewinds' two mastheads swept lazy circles around the constellations overhead, and the sea's calm surface broke into phosphorescent blue fire in our bow wave and wake. At last the grayness of early morning began washing out the stars in the east, and abruptly the sun hoisted itself over the ragged Coast Range rim, a burnished disc briefly battling the westering moon for dominance; then outshining it in dazzling brilliance.

We figured we had mastered the ocean and were bantering brags about our sea skill when the two-banger wheezed, hiccuped and died. A visual check put us about ten miles north of Depoe Bay. Mechanical diagnosis indicated malnutrition; the Frisco Standard was starving for fuel.

I dipsticked the tank and found it to be about half full. Clinging to the dipstick were flakes of rust-colored crud. The ocean swells had loosened scale and rust inside the tank and fouled the fuel lines. I disconnected all fuel lines, blew out the crud, reconnected, treadmilled the flywheel and kicked in the compression levers. She coughed, burped and died.

Again I grimaced through the fuel-line clearing, spewed a mouthful of gas over the side, foot-spun the flywheel, and the Frisco Standard ka-chucked into raucous action. A half dozen or so more times I had to revive the starving engine.

Meanwhile, time had sneaked past and the orange ball of the sun was perilously close to scuttling itself beyond the ocean's edge in the west. Ahead lay the strain of snaking *Tradewinds* from the open ocean to Depoe Bay's pipsqueak six-square-acre harbor through a skinny, rock-rimmed channel only twenty feet wide in places, and a hundred twisting yards in length.

Running the channel in daylight taxes the skill of veteran skippers. For a rank amateur to attempt it in darkness with a faltering engine was a brain-boggling prospect. And, at that time Depoe Bay had no Coast Guard station to signal for help.

The Depoe Bay sea buoy, a nautical mile west of the channel entrance, at last reared its moaning black-and-white bulk into our straining vision. As we neared the buoy, I sent one of the crewmen to the bow with a lariat-like line to lasso the buoy in case the Frisco Standard conked. It conked.

My sea-going cowboy lassoed a projection on the buoy with a bull's-eye thrust. Telling my crewmen to stay on deck to watch our buoy tether, I tackled the fuel lines one more weary time.

"Hit the deck; we got company!" yelled a crewman. I hit it, then gawked at a small, green-hulled fishing vessel bobbing nearby.

"Trouble?" asked the vessel's stocky, dark-visaged skipper, who proved to be veteran Depoe Bay fisherman, Everett "Butch" Munson. We poured out our woes.

Our sea-going Samaritan spat out a slug of tobacco juice and contemplated the darkening western sky. "About a half hour of daylight left," he said. "Untie from the whistler, heave me a line and I'll tow you in."

While one crewman cleared the buoy tether, made the towline fast and stood by it on the bow, the other handled the helm; and I sweated over the Frisco Standard hoping to avoid the ignominy of being towed into the harbor.

Fishing vessel entering turbulent Depoe Bay channel entrance. (Photo by author)

Half way to the channel entrance I got the damn thing perking, signaled Butch to cast off the tow line, and positioned my lariat-draped crewman on the bow. We wallowed toward the channel entrance on our own shaky power.

My heart was hammering harder than the Frisco Standard when I steered Tradewinds' bow into the narrow, surging entrance, coaxing and cussing the engine not to quit. It quit.

By crazy, dumb luck our own momentum and an insurging swell shoved the dead-engined craft through the twisting, jagged-edged channel toward the old Columbia River Packers Association dock, just inside the harbor.

Our bow cowboy heaved himself to hero status when he sent his makeshift lariat snaking toward the dock and plopped the noose squarely over a cleat. We hand-hauled the conked vessel to the dock and tied up. "One more damn fool made it," somebody on the dock sneered.

Stan Allyn aboard *Tradewinds* in Depoe Bay in 1938.
(from author's collection)

3. In the Beginning

Some sixteen million years ago, according to geologists, the seething bowels of the earth shot white-hot lava upward through a crust fissure, where it shattered a mountain and erupted in a cataclysmic explosion of hurtling molten rock near the present location of Cape Foulweather, four miles south of Depoe Bay.

Billions of tons of fiery lava spewed from the shattered mountain to the Pacific, where it flowed north and south several miles in an indescribable nightmare of fire, steam and titanic explosions. When the cold ocean water finally cooled the molten rock, it hardened to form the rugged coastline that exists to this day on Oregon's Lincoln County coast.

In the chaotic process, four miles north of Cape Foulweather, a narrow defile was formed in the hardening lava, extending from the ocean a hundred yards eastward to a rock-rimmed amphitheater-like area.

Through thousands of centuries the erosion from two streams pouring into this "amphitheater"—from the Coast Range Mountains in the east and the eternal pounding of the breakers through the small defile on the west—carved the narrow, rocky-gorge channel and picturesque, tree-edged harbor now famous as the pint-sized fishing port of Depoe Bay.

One of the first white men to get a close look at this wild, unexplored coast was famous English navigator-explorer, Captain James Cook. In early March, 1778, the 462-ton bark HMS *Resolution* and the smaller HMS *Discovery*, under Captain Cook's command, were beating through turbulent

Tree-surrounded Depoe Bay in 1912—before it had been used as a harbor. (Courtesy Lincoln County Historical Society)

Depoe Bay channel in 1912 before Highway 101 bridge was built and area developed. (Courtesy Lincoln County Historical Society)

seas and weather from the Sandwich Islands (now Hawaiian) in quest of the fabled Northwest Passage.

Cook hoped to win a twenty-thousand-pound prize the English parliament had offered to the mariner who discovered the strait which was then erroneously believed to cut through the North American continent linking the Pacific and Atlantic oceans.

At noon, March 6, 1778, Cook recorded in his journal: "We saw two seals and several whales," and at daybreak, March 7, he wrote: "The long looked for coast of New Albion was seen." (During an exploratory voyage two centuries earlier, English mariner, Sir Francis Drake, had given the name New Albion to the land that is now North America.)

Cook was looking exactly at what is now the Lincoln County coast in Oregon, and on March 7 he added to his journal: "The land appeared to be diversified with hills and valleys and almost everywhere covered with wood [evergreen forests]."

For days Cook's ships were buffeted by gale-driven rain, sleet and snow squalls, prompting him to write: "The land formed a point which I called Cape Foulweather from the very bad weather we met with." Cape Foulweather remains the headland's official charted name to this day and serves as a major navigational bearing point for vessels operating out of Depoe Bay.

Long before the coming of the white man, legend tells us, Indians paddled from the tiny bay in dugout canoes to hunt seals, sea lions and otter, and to fish for the salmon and rockfish that abound in the waters off this ruggedly beautiful coast. Mussels scraped from ocean-edge rocks added to the sea's bounty.

On meadows between the sea and the forest in the Depoe Bay area are kitchen middens or shell heaps, some an acre or more in extent, testifying to centuries of Indian feasts that took place here. Depoe Bay itself was named for an Indian —Chief White Buffalo Robe of the Siletz Indian tribe, whose name was changed later to Chief William "Charley" Depoe. The chief became the first land owner in the area when, in 1867, the government allotted him two hundred acres surrounding the tiny bay.

Chief White Buffalo Robe, of the Siletz Indian tribe, later acquired the name William Charley Depoe. In 1867 the "great white father" in Washington D.C., allotted him the two hundred acres now comprising the town and harbor which bear his name.

Hard-driving "Colonel" T. Egenton Hogg, described as a "sometimes colonel" during the Civil War, was indirectly responsible for changing the chief's life style and name. Boasting that he'd make Yaquina Bay, fourteen miles south of Depoe Bay, a "teaming mart of commerce to rival San Francisco", the "Colonel" punched the Oregon Pacific Railroad through the Coast Range Mountains from Corvallis to Yaquina City early in 1885.

Chief White Buffalo Robe took to making frequent treks over the twenty-mile trail south to Yaquina City, where he'd hang around the depot to watch the snorting iron horses puff in and out. Before many moons he was dubbed "Depot Charley."

One of the chief's sons decided that "Depot" lacked the sophistication befitting a full-blooded Indian chief, so he borrowed the French spelling from a French trapper he had befriended and changed the name to Depoe. The "Chief Charley Depoe" name stuck through the chief's last sunset. The naming of the bay and town in his honor constitutes an enduring memorial.

The first known white men to enter the hidden natural harbor were Dr. F.W. Vincent of Pendleton, Oregon, and his grandfather, who sailed north from Newport in 1878. Noticing a break in the shoreline, they lowered their sails and rowed their forty-foot craft through the twisting, rock-edged gorge. They were astonished to find themselves in the little cove, surrounded by sea cliffs and virgin forests.

Until well after the turn of the century, Depoe Bay—because of its inaccessibility—remained a secluded sylvan sea cove visited only by occasional venturesome hikers and horseback riders, and fishing vessels seeking refuge from storms.

Lincoln County was formed, February 20, 1893, when it was spliced together from hunks hacked off adjacent Polk and Benton counties. Transportation to the Lincoln County coast remained difficult. Early settlers journeyed to the area by horse and wagon over a military road, snaking sixty rough miles from Corvallis to Yaquina Bay.

After "Colonel" Hogg's railroad was put through, some rode it to Toledo, the first county seat, or to Yaquina City; then completed the last leg of the journey to the coast on

Mail driver Frank Johnson goads his team to full gallop to beat the next inrushing breaker as he rounds Yaquina John point near Waldport on the Lincoln County coast, illustrating early coastal transportation difficulties when accessible beaches were used. (Courtesy Lincoln County Historical Society)

Wood-burning Oregon Pacific passenger train at Yaquina City, its western terminus, where Chief White Buffalo Robe often trekked to hang around the depot and watch the iron horses snort in and out, thus being dubbed "Depot Charley," later changed by a son to the more sophisticated "Depoe." (From author's collection)

small river boats or on rafts and small boats poled and paddled down the Yaquina and Siletz rivers. Others voyaged to Siletz, Yaquina, and Alsea bays on small, coastal freight-passenger vessels.

Travel difficulties of the time are poignantly pointed up by the experiences of early Lincoln County coast settlers, Andrew and Anna Wisniewski. In 1895 they took "Colonel" Hogg's train to Toledo, jolted by horse and wagon over a rough, rutted road to the Indian reservation town of Siletz; then loaded bag and baggage on a raft Andrew built and paddled twenty-four miles down the corkscrewing Siletz River to the coast. There they took up a homestead.

Eventually they moved into a house built by Andrew from beach-combed lumber swept ashore from the decks of the foundering, storm-battered steam schooner *Minnie E. Kelton* in 1908. In 1923 Andrew and Anna's sons, Charley and Tony, hauled lumber and timbers from the beach and started construction of a house at then-remote Depoe Bay.

In 1926, Charley and Tony established themselves among Depoe Bay's first permanent residents when they married Lillian and Jessie Heaton—daughters of a Tillamook County dairy farmer—and moved into their completed home.

After Chief Depoe's death, his heirs sold his two hundred acres to a group of Newport investors "for a song." At the time, the buyers had scant hope of profiting from this inaccessible real estate, but in 1925 they sold it "lock, stock and bay" to a farsighted group of Portland businessmen for a reported ten thousand dollars.

The new owners, incorporated as the Sunset Investment Company, laid out streets and lots and set up shop to start selling. A few venturesome travelers who braved tough conditions to visit the area were but the ripple presaging the tidal wave of tourists who were to flood the town.

In 1926, construction crews completed a gracefully arched concrete bridge across the Depoe Bay channel. When the rough but passable Roosevelt Highway—predecessor to Coast Highway 101—was completed, things began to perk. Lots sold. Homes, shops and tourist facilities were built. Even Uncle Sam took note of the burgeoning town; on October 26, 1928, Depoe Bay's first post office was established, with Mrs. Paul "Edith" Baird serving as first postmaster.

Difficulties of Lincoln County coast travel before the coast highway was built are apparent in this 1912 photo of the first automobile to make the forty-seven-mile round trip between Newport and Siletz Bay. (Courtesy Lincoln County Historical Society)

Some of the cars at the Salmon Bake at Depoe Bay. aug 5-34

After the coast highway was completed in the late 1920s, visitors flocked to the Lincoln County coast, as evidenced by this photo taken during the Depoe Bay salmon bake, August 5, 1934. (From author's collection)

Pedestrian ferry, *T. M. Richardson*, pushing passenger-laden barge on the five-mile haul from the Yaquina City rail terminus to Newport; while Depoe Bay, thirteen miles north, remained an isolated sea cove until completion of the coast highway in the late 1920s. (From author's collection)

Before the coast highway was built, passengers and freight were largely transported to and from Lincoln County ports on small coastal craft such as this schooner shown just after docking at Newport. (Courtesy Lincoln County Historical Society)

Two-lane, channel-spanning Highway 101 bridge at Depoe Bay, shortly after its completion in 1926. Small oar-powered boats moored to rocks braved Depoe Bay's narrow, rock-rimmed channel to take persons deep-sea fishing on the Pacific in early days. (From author's collection)

Scaffolding used in widening channel-spanning Highway 101 bridge in Depoe Bay in 1940. (From author's collection)

By the mid-1930s, fish-buying firms had installed docks
and receiving stations in the tiny harbor, and a score or
more of fishing vessels were running the gamut of the narrow
rock-ragged channel to fish the offshore waters. Also, a half
dozen or so craft had started making passenger deep-sea
fishing trips. Mostly they were commercial fishing vessels
using heavy, hand-operated gear worked by crewmen, who
divided the catch among those aboard.

The Coast Guard took heed of the little port's increasing
activity by installing navigational range markers ashore and
a whistle buoy a nautical mile offshore to help guide mariners to and through the channel.

But the toughest hazards remained a narrow channel and
a shallow harbor. The terrible stress of steering a plunging
vessel through inrushing seas from the open ocean into the
roiling narrow channel—with its jagged rock fangs reaching
out for vessels to gore—strained the nerves and skill of the
most experienced skippers.

Tough, too, were the channel and bay's depth—or lack
thereof. At low tide there simply was not enough water to
navigate in either the channel or bay, and every vessel went
hard aground, leaving the nested vessels leaning cheek-to-
jowl against each other, like fallen dominoes.

This, then, was the pint-sized port from which I was determined to sail to my deep-sea fishing fortune on the often
unpeaceful Pacific.

4. Wild Boar's Nest

The morning after *Tradewinds'* shaky, dead-engine arrival, we gulped a good breakfast at the Depoe Bay blufftop Spouting Horn Restaurant, and my erstwhile crewmen headed up the highway for Portland.

I cased the little town; then went to the docks. My reception by Depoe Bay fishermen was considerably less than cordial. They resented a young city punk's invading "their bay" and "their ocean." However, I won the friendship of a fish company dock worker by helping him fit a stubborn dock timber to its slot; then he bullied a space where I was able to moor *Tradewinds.*

Finally I slugged it out with the Frisco Standard, cleaning the crud out of the gas tank and fuel lines for starters. After that I took a crack at the carburetor, removed it to the deck and began fumbling it apart.

From time to time Depoe Bay fishermen stopped briefly, from a wary distance, to stare glumly and silently at my labors. You'd have thought I had leprosy.

After while a slender, weather-worn fellow, who I later learned was veteran fisherman, Art Lannegan, evidently decided my city-slicker malady was not infectious and ventured aboard. He grunted a string of salty oaths, then gathered up my dismembered carburetor and took off, mumbling something about "G!!**##! + + stupid city guys." In a short time he quietly re-appeared with the re-assembled carburetor, hooked it up, and motioned me to spin the flywheel.

I spun. The Frisco Standard barked a couple of times; then settled to its normal, noisy ka-chuck, ka-chuck.

The engine's steady pounding created a miraculous transition in my benefactor. His seemingly frozen frown thawed to a wide, gap-toothed grin. I grabbed his rough hand and pumped till his jowls jiggled.

The antique Frisco Standard's racket wrought further miracles. From all over the dock area it drew fishermen to *Tradewinds*, the way a magnet attracts nails. Shortly they were crowded around the Frisco Standard—listening, pointing, making suggestions.

Finally I shut it off. Then, chattering and joking like lifelong shipmates, we trooped topside to the Bayside Tavern, where I sprung for beers all around. I was "in."

As time went on, other fishermen gradually began to stop by to chat and offer advice on ocean fishing. They gave me hints on locating schooled salmon, such as trolling around feeding sea birds and working tide rips and plankton-laden, brownish-colored water.

They showed me how to rig deep "meat lines," using twenty or more pounds of lead on heavy line sprouting up to a half dozen leaders and lures per line—standard rig for most Depoe Bay passenger deep-sea fishing vessels at that time. Not wanting to spark a local revolution, I later secretly bought and sneaked aboard six inexpensive rods and reels with which to offer hoped-for future passengers a semblance of sportfishing.

Other fishermen warned me not to sail when heavy westerly swells were rolling in, pointing out that westerlies slam the channel head-on and bash it to a seething boil of crashing breakers. They told me how to enter the channel if caught in heavy westerly swells that might build suddenly while I was at sea, pointing out that heavy swells usually come in rushes of seven or more, and after the rushes there's usually a brief "flat spot."

In this situation they advised approaching the channel to within a hundred or so yards; then heaving to and waiting until the rushes of big blisters rolled under my vessel and crashed through the channel. "Then get to H--- in on the flat spot before the next rush," they emphasized.

Best advice of all when the channel's really bad, they said, is to ride it out in deep water offshore till the heavy swells subside; then go in. Almost any vessel will bring you through safely if you keep it in deep water, they counseled, adding that most vessels come to grief when their skippers, trying to flee storms and heavy seas, take their craft into shallow, breaker-bashed harbor entrances.

One who gave me advice was a jolly, heavy-set charter fisherman named Dick Earl, skipper of the passenger deep-sea fishing vessel *Pauline B*. Later that summer I was to watch in helpless horror as an irate passenger shot him dead.

Ruth came along dockside while I was squatting on *Trade-winds'* afterdeck, rigging gear so intently I was unaware of her presence till her slight throat-clearing swiveled my gaze to her.

Ruth (sketch by author)

"Permission to come aboard, skipper?" she asked, throwing me a mock salute.

The author's twenty-eight-foot converted Columbia River gillnetter *Tradewinds* under sail off Depoe Bay. (From author's collection)

In my haste to jerk upright I banged my rear on the gunnel overhang and nearly fell flat. Regaining my balance, I offered her the assistance of my hand and nearly fell flat again when I got a good look at this dazzling creature.

Her long, shining cornsilk-blond hair, lively blue eyes and creamy complexion highlighted her Nordic beauty. Her lips were parted in a provocative smile, and as she took my proffered hand and bent to climb over the gunnel, the bright yellow sweater she was wearing was hard put to contain the thrust of her full young breasts. Nor did her yellow slacks camouflage her slender, well-formed legs as she sat on the deck and laced her fingers together around her knees.

"You darned near fell for me—literally," she kidded in a seductive, throaty voice that rattled my keelson from stem to stern. "I'm Ruth Albertson, and my fisherman brother, Mel, told me about your plans to desert the big city for life on the briny." In the animated conversation that followed, I learned that she was eighteen and a waitress at a Depoe Bay restaurant.

As she left, an hour and fourteen sea stories later, my zeal to show off my soon-to-be prowess on the sea nudged me into inviting her to sail on my first deep-sea fishing voyage —an invitation I was to regret.

In late May, *Tradewinds* was rigged, ready and ship-shape, and on a bright, calm Sunday morning, with Ruth tagging along, I prowled the crowded Depoe Bay bridge sidewalk and talked four trusting people into plunking out two dollars each (the going rate at that time) to sail aboard *Tradewinds* on our first four-hour, deep-sea fishing trip.

After herding my passengers to the dock, then across nested fishing vessels to *Tradewinds*, I spun the flywheel and the Frisco Standard cooperated with a first-spin start. I safely threaded the little craft through the calm, rocky channel, steered her westward over gentle gray-green swells and started looking for salmon signs. The advice handed me by my fishermen advisers paid off. About three miles off-shore I spotted a big swirl of gulls wheeling, circling and diving to the sea's undulating surface.

Ruth, shipshape and lovely in a saucy-blue yacht cap, middy and bell-bottom jeans, handed the troll-rigged rods to our anglers, while I homed in on the birds, slowed to what I hoped the right trolling speed; I put *Tradewinds* on a circling course around the berserk birds as my advisers had suggested.

Then I left the wheel, and while Ruth helped the anglers pay out their lines I lowered the outriggers and successfully, if slowly, eased out the heavy, deep lines, one from each outrigger.

The squawking, screeching birds all but drowned out the shouts of the anglers when two of them hooked salmon. Both played their scrappy-fish beauties to the stern like experts, and I promptly knocked them off the hooks with the gaff.

While this was going on, *Tradewinds*, with no one at the helm, kept circling—tighter and tighter and tighter. By the time I yanked the helm to a straight course, both outrigger lines were tending toward each other under the hull, snarled together and doing the St. Vitus dance. I kicked the Frisco Standard out of gear, and as we drifted to a stop, rolling gently in the easy swell, I grabbed the haul-in line leading from the stern to the starboard outrigger line and started hauling it in, but it fetched up solid. Then I tried the port line. Solid.

That's when the anglers started hollering that their rod and reel lines had dropped straight down and were hung up. I had to do something quick, even if it was wrong—which it was.

I lashed a knife to the end of a boat hook, reached out with it, and hacked at the port outrigger line. It parted with a zing. I next tried pulling the starboard line, gaining a hard-won fathom or so. Then I started grunting in handfuls of what had to be the worst outrigger and sport tackle tangle in the annals of deep-sea fishing.

Foot by sweating foot I muscled most of the line in; then it hung up solid on the propeller, rudder, or some other protuberance under the hull. I strained with a mighty heave, wrenched the line loose and toppled flat on my back amid the mess on deck—ensnarled in hooks, lines and leaders. Tangled in the cocoon of snarled fishline were two strangled silverside salmon.

Ruth helped me claw myself clear, and I tackled the mess in an effort to extricate the salmon. Ruth suggested that it might be prudent to head for port and clear the mess at the dock. So, we headed in, frayed lines and leaders streaming from under the counter in our wake.

A half hour later we moored; and our anglers, muttering under their breath, crossed the nested vessels to the dock, heading glumly topside with their two gear-gouged salmon.

Ruth patted my shoulder. "Anyway, skipper," she consoled, "we didn't get skunked."

5. Calm To Killer

Sadder but wiser.

That trite but true platitude caught me squarely amidships as I labored repairing and rerigging the gear we had snafued. While I worked, the thought hounded me that Ruth would have no use for me following my bungling sea exhibition. A couple of days later when my brain jabbed me into the thought that a shakedown fishing trip without passengers would be wise, I goaded myself into inviting Ruth, half expecting her to slam her cottage door in my face when I knocked.

"I'll bring a lunch!" She shot me her reply without pause. A short time later we were churning westward over still-gentle ground swells.

On this and following trips I learned much. We found and worked feeding birds, trolling their outer perimeter in easy long circles so as not to foul the gear or sound the school by barging through its center.

I got hep to the disaster of chopping down on the fish with the gaff, like a logger felling a tree, and acquired the knack of thrusting the gaff under the fish's head and lifting up and aboard in one quick, unbroken motion.

I learned to work salmon-rich tide rips—the frontal edges of huge masses of tidal water moving almost always from offshore toward the beach. Their roiling, miles-long frontal edges, I discovered, usually extend slantwise from southwest to northeast and bulldoze through the sea plankton, minnows, seaweed and all manner of flotsam, which provides fertile feeding for the salmon.

And I got wise to the trick of following gulls and other sea birds winging in the same direction. They are usually bee-lining toward shoals of minnows, with salmon underneath. Lacking birds or tide rips, plankton-rich brown water is usually crammed with minnows feeding on the plankton, and salmon munching the minnows.

If I failed to find any of these salmon signs, I learned to drop a lanyard-lashed sea thermometer over the side and get the water temperature, seeking the fifty-to-fifty-four degree temperature that experienced fishermen advised was best for salmon.

The anglers came; the salmon bit. *Tradewinds* frolicked over the Pacific's heaving, sun-dappled surface to and from the fishing areas without foul-up. The future for the sea and me looked bright.

It was hard to believe that in the span of a few hours, this same sparkling, bountiful ocean could change to a raging killer. I was to learn of one tragic example of the ocean's treachery the next day.

That morning the splatter of wind-driven rain against *Tradewinds*, at dock, jarred me awake. Whipped by a brisk southwest wind, the Pacific growled its warning of heavy seas, forcing all vessels to remain in port. Shortly after I had hoisted myself gloomily out of my bunk and crawled into damp clothes, Ruth breezed aboard.

"Hit the deck, skipper," she commanded. "I'll give you the grand tour of the town." Her dripping, yellow sou'wester and slicker did not dampen her cheery smile or disguise the splendid young body beneath.

She built me a quick bacon, eggs, and coffee breakfast aboard, then towed me topside and north through the town.

"Behold!—one of Depoe Bay's claims to fame," she shouted, pointing to a geyser of sea water shooting fifteen fathoms skyward from what appeared to be the top of a solid volcanic-rock, ocean-edge bluff, across from the town's north-end business district.

"Our famous Spouting Horns!" she proclaimed, explaining that heavy seas pound into submerged, nature-carved tunnels, then blast skyward through sea-carved vertical shafts.

Depoe Bay's famous spouting horns gush over a hundred feet skyward through sea-carved holes in rocky, ocean-edge bluff. Early developers came within a squirt of filling the now-famous horn openings with concrete to prevent sea water from spraying the nearby town. (Photo by author)

"Like Yellowstone's Old Faithful, the Spouting Horns bring great publicity to Depoe Bay all over the nation and then some," she said, wiping rain drips from her perky nose and chin. "Now I'll tell you something funny."

"Early residents recall how the Sunset Investment Company's Depoe Bay developers came within a squirt of eliminating our famous attraction. They were about to fill the vertical Spouting Horn shafts with concrete to stop the sea water from spraying over the highway and town," she chuckled, "and decided against it only after fervent last-ditch pleadings by one publicity-conscious member of the group."

Ruth tugged me through the drenching swirl of sea and rain water to a nearby stone monument atop the sea-battered bluff. "This shows how cruel the sea can be," she said, pointing somberly to a bronze plaque on the monument.

The legend engraved on the sea-tarnished plaque states that the monument was erected in memory of Depoe Bay fishermen Roy Bower and Jack Chambers, who on October 4, 1936, gave their lives in a heroic effort to rescue storm-imperiled fellow fishermen off Depoe Bay—a story in itself.

6. "A Breaker Was Busting over Her"

The following few days I yarned with Depoe Bay fishermen about the Bower-Chambers tragedy, including a confab with Ernest McQueen, whose imperiled vessel they were attempting to assist when calamity struck. Ironically, McQueen steered his battered vessel safely to port the morning following the disaster.

From it all I pieced together events leading up to and following the fatal rescue try . . .

A steep, green sea heaved the thirty-six-foot troller *Cara Lou* to its frothing crest, then dropped it into the yawning trough beyond. The sea had been building steadily all through that cloud-shrouded October fourth in 1936, and as the watery, late-afternoon sun crawled toward the ragged horizon, a gray pall of fog began settling over the Pacific's heaving surface off Depoe Bay.

Aboard the *Cara Lou*, Skipper Roy Bower hurriedly hauled in his salmon-trolling gear, housed the outriggers, and shoved the throttle ahead. Smashing through curling crests and plunging troughs, the *Cara Lou* clawed alongside the wallowing sea buoy, where Bower set his course for Depoe Bay's channel entrance, a mile to the eastward.

Holding to a deep-water course between thundering combers on North and South reefs, he maneuvered his bucking craft to the breaker-bashed channel entrance, waited for the flat spot between rushes, then skillfully snaked the vessel through the channel's churning hundred-yard length to the quiet safety of the tiny harbor.

He quickly tied the *Cara Lou* to the dock and hurried to the channel-spanning Highway 101 bridge to watch anxiously with fellow fisherman, Jack Chambers, as all but one of the vessels of the Depoe Bay fishing Fleet churned into the channel to the safety of the harbor. The twenty-five-foot troller *Norwester* was still at sea.

As Bower and Chambers stared into the gathering fog, their anxiety deepened, for they knew that if the frail craft didn't reach port soon, it would be trapped by fog and darkness in the mounting seas.

They also knew that on board the imperiled troller was not only its skipper, McQueen, but also two fourteen-year-old boys: Walter McQueen, the skipper's son, and Gene McLaughlin, a guest. Abruptly Bower pointed to a spray-drenched blur that was the *Norwester*, laboring toward the sea buoy. Then the fog swirled onto the ocean's surface in a black mass, blotting out all vision.

"Let's go!" yelled Bower. Chambers was already on his way. They raced down the steps to the dock, started the *Cara Lou's* engine, cast off and slammed through the surging channel toward the position where they'd glimpsed the *Norwester*. Fifty feet offshore the fog swallowed them.

McQueen described the tragic events that followed:

"I had tied to the sea buoy and was going to ride it out there till morning. All a sudden the *Cara Lou* comes busting out of the fog, and Bower and Chambers holler at me to cast off and follow them in.

"I cut loose and followed them on a northeasterly heading for about five minutes. The seas kept getting steeper and steeper, and then one big one busted clean over my vessel and broached us broadside.

"I'll never know how we missed capsizing, or how that danged engine kept running, but we slammed out of it in one piece and I headed back to the sea buoy and tied up. It was dark then with a black-out fog.

"Last I saw of the *Cara Lou* she had swung beam-on to the seas and a breaker was busting over her. I didn't know till I came in next morning that Bower and Chambers hadn't made it. God, I wish I could have done something to help."

When neither vessel returned to port that night, fishermen aboard other vessels attempted to batter their way to sea through the rampaging channel to search for the missing vessels but, each time, the thrashing combers clubbed them to a standstill, and they were barely able to get back to the safety of the harbor. Then the tide dropped below navigable depth, shutting off further search attempts.

Throughout the black night, fishermen and townsfolk patrolled the rocky shoreline in the hope of spotting or hearing something. By the next morning the sea had moderated, but the cotton-wool fog still clung to the sea's dark surface.

Suddenly, anxious watchers on the highway bridge heard the stutter of a boat's engine, and a hazy blur grew to the little *Norwester* struggling toward the channel entrance.

McQueen wrestled his plunging craft through the channel to the harbor and tied up.

Fishermen pounded down the stairs to the dock, informed the shocked McQueen that the *Cara Lou* had not returned, got a quick report of where he'd last seen the missing vessel, and got underway in their own vessels to fan out over the Pacific's fog-shrouded surface in a desperate search.

They found the battered hulk of the *Cara Lou* drifting awash two miles northwest of Depoe Bay. Bower's body was aboard, tangled in the rigging. Chambers was floating nearby in a life preserver. He had died from exposure.

A few days later, fishing vessels carried relatives and friends of the drowned fishermen onto the Pacific, where their ashes and flowers were scattered on the water in a brief ceremony.

Later, Bower and Chambers were posthumously awarded the Carnegie medal for heroism.

The author beside granite monument overlooking the Pacific at Depoe Bay, erected by the State of Oregon in tribute to fishermen Roy Bower and Jack Chambers, who gave their lives in an effort to assist a storm-imperiled fellow fisherman. (From author's collection)

7. Jaws

The shark locked fins with us in mid-June. . . . We were trolling into a light southerly chop about four miles southwest of Depoe Bay. Fishing was slow and I had set *Tradewinds* on a steady course and stepped to the after-deck, where I lit off my pipe and was telling sea stories to my anglers.

Halfway through one of my yarns I was cut off abruptly when one angler's mouth flapped agape and his eyes popped open, porthole size.

Wh - wh - what's that?" he stammered, pointing to a spot forward of the starboard bow.

I swiveled to the direction of his pointing and stiffened in shock.

Slicing through the sea's green surface on a near-collision course, a few yards ahead, was a huge, black, yard-high triangular dorsal fin. Twenty or more feet behind the dorsal, the scimitar-shaped top of the shark's tail fin weaved slowly from side to side, propelling its hideous bulk toward us. I dived into the wheelhouse and wrenched the helm to port.

The monster came plowing down our starboard side on a parallel opposite course not a foot from the hull. We stared in petrified awe as its huge head surged into view just beneath the surface alongside, its monstrous jaws open like an enormous scoop. Its massive body was longer than *Tradewinds*.

The shark cleared the hull, but we stood braced for the shock if it fouled our trolling lines. Suddenly the heavy starboard outrigger lines stretched and jerked in a demon's dance. The spruce outrigger pole bent back slowly, inexorably, to near breaking strain.

The terrific stress hauled *Tradewinds* around to starboard, totally nullifying the pull of rudder and propeller—but the behemoth swam on, seemingly oblivious of its straining tow.

Gradually it veered across our wake, and in the process swam into the anglers' sport lines. Their yells startled a nearby group of resting gulls into terrified flight.

I prayed to the gods of the seas, and they took heed. As though guided by an unseen hand, the fishing lines started rising toward the surface, and one by one they slithered across the giant shark's back and plummeted back into the sea without snagging. Total loss was a few lures and leaders—though lost, too, was our zeal for further fishing. We brought in the gear and hauled to port.

I hotfooted it to Ruth's and exploded the shark tale. Her "ho-hum" attitude about decked me.

"Yes, skipper," she drawled, affecting a massive yawn. "Basking shark. One of the world's biggest fish. I've seen lots of them from my brother's boat."

But she confessed that she, too, was scared out of her wits when she saw her first basking shark; the next day, she bought a book on sea creatures to find out more about basking and other sharks.

She pulled the book from a shelf and read excerpts:

"Basking sharks reach a length of fifty feet and several tons in weight. Among the world's largest fish they are topped only by whale sharks, which have been reported at an astounding seventy feet. . . .

"Basking sharks are so named because they appear to be basking just under the surface, but actually they are plodding along with their giant jaws agape gulping the tiny marine organisms they feed on. . . .

"Neither basking nor whale sharks can eat large objects because of the tiny teeth with which they're equipped."

They're monstrous examples of nature's irony, I learned, for dangerous as they look, these largest of all fishes are considered harmless as hares. Gear damage they cause now and then is by sheer blundering accident.

Twenty-foot great white shark, one of the most voracious known sea species. Great whites are seldom seen in Pacific Northwest waters; while basking sharks to fifty feet in length frequent the area but feed on small marine organisms and are considered harmless. (From author's collection)

Gaping jaws of one of the giant sharks that periodically prowl Pacific Northwest waters. (From author's collection)

Ruth read on:

"The great white shark, often called man-eater, is considered the swiftest and most voracious of all sharks. It grows to forty or more feet in length, and its mouth is studded with several sets of large razor-sharp teeth, one row in back of another. When teeth break off, spares work their way forward to replace them. . . .

"All sharks are unpredictable and will swallow almost anything. One shark captured off an Australian dock had in its stomach half a ham, several legs of mutton, the hindquarters of a pig, the head and forelegs of a bulldog with a rope tied around its neck, a quantity of horseflesh, a piece of cloth and a ship's scraper. In the belly of another caught in the Adriatic Sea were, among other things, three overcoats, a nylon raincoat and an automobile license plate. . . .

"In a bizarre incident in Australia," Ruth read on, "a big tiger shark coughed up incriminating evidence in a 1935 murder case. The shark was caught and put in a Sydney aquarium as a tourist attraction. Eight days later it disgorged a human arm with an identifying tattoo on it.

"Medical examiners discovered that the arm had been cut off with a knife, not by the shark's teeth, and turned it over to police, who traced it to a boxer who had been reported missing two weeks before. Checking further they found that the boxer had apparently been murdered by fellow conspirators when their scheme to wreck a yacht and collect the insurance failed.

"The suspected murderers had evidently succeeded in jamming all the body but the arm in a box; so they cut it off and heaved it overboard, followed by the boxed body. In a one-in-a-million shot, the shark swallowed the arm, was caught, and later produced the evidence."

Each year throughout the world, several dozen proven shark attacks on human beings that result in death or maiming take place, and numerous hairbreadth escapes are reported.

Blue sharks harass Pacific Northwest fishermen more than any other of the some two hundred and fifty species that roam the seas. Blues average four to six feet in length— small, as sharks go—but they're salmon feeders and they're smart.

They'll laze along in the wake of a fishing vessel until a salmon is hooked. Then they'll highball toward the hooked fish, and it's a race whether the fisherman or the shark gets it. Often the fisherman ends up with half a salmon, or the head, or a bitten-off leader.

Many times I've gaffed tooth-raked salmon right out of sharks' jaws, smack against the transom.

The unusual experience of a Carson City, Nevada, angler points it up dramatically. . . .

8. Lucky Thirteen

"Smith's the name, Bob 'Wrong-Type' Smith, from Carson City," he said, locking my hand in a grip that sparked immediate respect. He had just climbed aboard at the dock with a look of determination and zestful anticipation. His short but wiry appearance and the square thrust of his jaw gave the impression of competent strength and the ability to cope with tough situations. His experience on the Pacific was to prove those qualities and tax them sorely.

Overhead, first daylight was squeezing the last glimmer from the stars as the sun hoisted itself toward the tree-studded Coast Range rim.

In the west, gauzy light penetrated a film of early-morning mist to reveal long Pacific ground swells with no surface chop, giving promise of fine fishing. Shortly we'd be out there trolling for salmon.

"Here's how I got the 'Wrong-Type' handle hung on me," confided Bob, broadsiding my salmon thoughts. "Last fall some guys and I went deer hunting in the hills outside of Carson City. We got snowed out with a freak unseasonal snow storm, and I didn't get a shot at a deer.

"So we packed out of there, grabbed our shotguns and headed for the marshlands to hunt ducks. I was hunkered on a log with my shotgun across my knees, and damned if a big buck didn't saunter past within fifty yards. I couldn't do a thing about it without getting arrested for shooting a deer with a shotgun. And I didn't get any ducks.

"Later I decided to take a crack at deep-sea fishing; so my family and I drove to Newport Beach, California, and out I

45

went. There were twenty or so fishermen aboard, and they
were all catching fish—except me.

"Finally, just before the trip was over, I hooked what felt
to me like the biggest critter in the sea. I ground away and
finally got it to the surface and the deck-hands gaffed
aboard a four-foot shovelnose shark—worthless as a divot
on a duck pond.

"Now, Stan, I'm gonna make this early-morning salmon
trip and break my jinx," he chuckled, rubbing his hands in
confident exultation.

"Looks good, Wrong-Ty. . .er, I mean Bob," I encour-
aged. "No wind and the bite's been hot on this early four-
hour trip."

"Only four hours?" he questioned. "Is that time enough
to get out there and find'em?"

I assured him that it was, for the reason that unlike nearly
every other port in the world, sailing from Depoe Bay does
not require a long harbor run, and there's no bar to cross
to reach the fishing areas.

I cast off and we eased through the channel, lifted to the
first ground swell, slid down its backside, and snorted west.

Bob was standing beside me, and I explained to him the
salmon signs we look for. Two or so miles to the west, I
pointed out the churning line of a promising-looking tide
rip. While we churned toward it, I got Bob and the other
five anglers rigged out. Just short of the rip I slowed to our
normal two-knot trolling speed, eased into the rip and
trolled southwest through its roiling center.

"Strike! Fish on! Wow!" The shouts of the anglers erupted
almost immediately.

Hook-up, reel, thump! Bedlam! I was hard put to keep
up with gaffing and re-setting lines, and I lost all track of
time. Then suddenly all went quiet. The rip petered out.
The bite stopped. Minnow-crammed birds settled on the
water, sea-washing their bills and preening their feathers.

During the breather I took stock. Twelve shiny silver-side
salmon gleamed in the fish box. I asked Bob how many he'd
boated.

"None," he mumbled. "Typical 'Wrong-Type' Smith
luck."

"Shark!" yelled one of the anglers, pointing astern.

Left to right: Bob Jarrell holding ten-pound silverside salmon he boated during charter trip off Depoe Bay; Norm Hendrickson, mate aboard charter vessel, holding blue shark Jarrell also caught, and Jill Churchill holding half a silverside she boated after Jarrell's blue shark chomped off its back half while she was playing it in. (Photo by author)

Pacing us in the wake was the triangular, dark-blue fin of a blue shark.

"Hook Up!" Bob bellowed.

A hooked silverside salmon (alias, coho, depending on the area you're in) will usually rocket to the surface and fight in a series of leaps, cartwheels and helter-skelter rushes. But a chinook (alias, king) will almost always head for the bottom of the sea, like a sounding whale. Bob's did that, rasping great gobs of line from his reel in powerful thrusts. Figuring it for a big chinook in the forty-pound-plus category, I cut our speed to a crawl.

Bob handled the gear like an expert, easing the star drag to let the monster take line till it tired; then tightening up to reel and gain a little. Give, take, pump, ease off, cinch up, reel. Time faded into forever.

I had one of the anglers stand by me in the stern with the spare gaff.

Forever ended. Bob battled it to the surface at the stern. We drove the gaffs home and heaved aboard a six-foot blue shark!

"Here we go again," croaked Bob in a gasping gurgle that was to be his last intelligible utterance during the trip.

Time had run out. We hauled in the gear, and I rammed the throttle to full ahead toward port. Finally I summoned the courage to glance back at Bob. He'd collapsed against the bulwark and sat glassy-eyed, mumbling to himself, plucking fish scales from the deck.

At the dock I unloaded the fish, including Bob's blue shark, and asked a local lad on the dock to dress out the salmon. As an afterthought I told him to open up the shark's belly to see what it had been feeding on.

He did so, let out a yell, and told me to come look. In the shark's stomach lay a medium-sized but respectable chinook salmon—intact. Dressed out and washed, it proved to be bright and firm, not yet eroded by the shark's stomach acid. Obviously Bob had hooked it and a split second later the shark had gulped it down whole.

It was number thirteen salmon of the trip, and it broke Bob's jinx.

9. He Shot the Skipper Dead

July blasted in on a screeching northwest wind that ripped the seas's surface to a chaos of frothing whitecaps. It also blasted a horrible memory in my brain. Before the month was out, I was to witness the murder of a fellow charter-vessel skipper.

For three days the nor'wester howled and hammered, but on July fourth, as if in deference to the founding fathers, it finally subsided. Fishermen and skippers quickly filled the void left by the dying wind and erupted in an uproar racket of their own.

Early in the day they began upholding the ages-old reputation of sailors as two-fisted drinkers. By mid-morning they appeared to have downed enough booze to float the entire Depoe Bay fishing fleet.

The harbor could best be described as one big, roaring volcano of shouting, laughing, singing, cussing fishermen. Their racket was punctuated by the explosions of fireworks and the splashes of those falling in the drink.

Tradewinds and I appeared to be the only vessel-skipper team capable of navigating, and with six anglers aboard we braved a course through the threatening human tumult, making it to the comparative quiet of the Pacific. By the time we returned to port with our catch four hours later, the harbor was quiet as a clam at high tide. The celebrants were sleeping off whale-size hangovers.

The weather held fair until mid-July, when swirling black fog rode in on another nor'wester, blanketing the sea in sepulcher gloom that kept all vessels harbor-bound. To the amazement of Depoe Bay boatmen, on July 17 the charter-vessel *Pauline B.* plowed seaward into the brooding murk with a youngish, stylishly dressed couple as its only passengers.

Butch Munson, who had assisted me on the day of my trouble-plagued Depoe Bay arrival, was aboard the *Pauline B.* as mate, and Dick Earl, who I had met soon after my arrival, was skipper. It was to be his last voyage on this earth.

The *Pauline B.* did not return that day or during the following black night.

Early next morning a friend and I were double-mooring *Tradewinds* at a south-side dock prior to driving to Portland. The fog still hung over the ocean like a shroud, and as we worked we were astonished to see the *Pauline B.* come ghosting through the murky channel and moored at her dock on the north side of the bay.

We watched the well-dressed couple disembark and head topside up the steep steps, with skipper, Dick Earl, and mate, Butch, following. A white sport coat worn by the male passenger attracted our attention because of its incongruity as attire for a seafaring venture. That coat was to figure prominently as evidence in its wearer's defense at his murder trial later.

Shortly we climbed the south-side steps to the highway shoulder where my Olds was parked. (A friend had earlier driven it from Portland for me.) But, the Olds wouldn't start. Dead battery.

We shoved the car north across the bridge, alternately pushing and slapping it in gear. No luck. Just beyond the north end of the bridge we stopped for a breather in front of the Spouting Horn Inn.

Parked at an angle against the curb directly across the highway to the west was the nattily dressed couples' green Dodge. Standing beside the open right front door in deep conversation were Skipper Earl, Butch and the couple.

Butch hollered across the highway to ask if we needed a hand to help push. At our nod he trotted over.

I have had no schooling in law and don't pretend to be a "sea lawyer." The events that follow I have set down exactly as I saw and heard them.

Anchored at far right in this photo of Depoe Bay taken in 1938 is the author's converted gillnetter *Tradewinds*. Moored alongside dock is the charter vessel *Pauline B.*, skippered by Dick Earl, whose murder by a charter passenger was witnessed by the author. (From author's collection)

To protect their inherent rights, instead of using the couples real names, I will refer to the man as "Stiddly Nielsen,"
and to his lady companion as "the girl."

The three of us had just started pushing the Olds when we
heard Earl's and Nielsen's voices rise to shouting pitch. Our
gaze snapped in their direction just in time to see Nielsen
raise a .38 caliber revolver he'd snatched from his car's
glove compartment and fire four shots at Earl at close range.

He then shoved the girl into the passenger seat, raced
around the car, leaped into the driver's seat, slammed into
gear-grinding reverse to the highway, rammed to forward
gear and roared south in a blast of exhaust smoke.

We rushed to Earl, who lay sprawled face down on the
gravel sidewalk. Gently as possible we rolled him onto his
back, ripped his jacket and shirt open and did what we
could to help him. Gasping gurgles brought bloody spittle
from his mouth, and blood bubbled from three holes in his
chest. He died in about a minute.

The revolver's sharp reports jerked special policeman,
Harley Youngblood, from sound sleep in the nearby Cliff
House Restaurant (since destroyed by fire).

Strapping a holstered revolver over his hastily thrown-on
clothes, he sprinted from the Cliff House, got quick information from us, leaped into his car parked nearby, and
rocketed south in hot pursuit.

We later learned that he overtook the fleeing couple four
miles south atop Cape Foulweather, took them into custody
without resistance, and drove them to the Lincoln County
seat at Toledo, where Nielsen was booked for murder in the
first degree, and the girl was held as an accomplice. Both
were lodged in the county jail pending trial.

As eye witnesses to the shooting, my friend and I were
summoned to testify at the trial later that year.

Nielsen's reputedly wealthy parents hired for his defense
three attorneys, said to be the smartest criminal lawyers
in the state. These lawyers coaxed, cajoled and bored into
witnesses in a manner appalling to us in our first experience
with the United States judicial system. It appeared as
though they had paid off witnesses to distort the facts. Some
of their "witnesses" were nowhere near when the early-

morning shooting took place, yet they testified as to things that simply did not happen.

Nielsen claimed that the reason for the shooting-climaxed argument was that Skipper Earl and Butch had tried to molest his lady friend while they were at sea; yet it was brought out by the prosecution that Nielsen was married, had left his wife at their valley home and "stepped out on her" for a lark at the coast with his erstwhile girlfriend.

The prosecution claimed that the shooting stemmed from an argument between Nielsen and Skipper Earl over the amount Nielsen was to pay for the cruise.

Another bizarre twist thrown into the case was Butch Munson's statement that the *Pauline B's* ill-fated voyage was made for the ostensible purpose of Skipper Earl's marrying Nielsen and the girl at sea, a rite totally outside his legal qualifications.

Finally, the defense attorneys triumphantly produced their key exhibit—the white sport coat worn by Nielsen before and during the shooting. They pointed to a char-edged hole in the coat and stated that Earl had grabbed Nielsen's revolver and shot at the defendant first. The bullet, they claimed, had gone through the coat, as evidenced by the hole, but miraculously missed Nielsen's body.

A struggle ensued, they maintained, with dramatic arm gyrations, and Nielsen managed to wrest the revolver from Earl and then shot him in self defense.

In refutation the prosecution presented ballistics experts and other authorities learned in such matters, who emphatically stated that intensive laboratory tests had conclusively proved that the hole in the coat had been made by a lighted cigarette burning through the fabric from the inside. A bullet, they pointed out, would have penetrated the coat from the outside.

The prosecutor promptly theorized that during Nielsen's dash from the shooting site to Cape Foulweather, he was hatching his defense and deliberately burned the hole through his coat with a cigarette in order to claim that it was made by a bullet fired by Earl.

We testified for the prosecution that in our close view of the shooting we did not see the gun in Earl's hand, did not see a struggle, but we *did* see Nielsen point his revolver at Earl at close range and fire.

The jurors, honest-appearing folk from throughout Lincoln County, seemed to be cowed by the defense attorneys' theatrics, which left them feeling sorry for this poor young man accused of murder in the first degree. Apparently small credence was accorded our eye-witness testimony.

The verdict: Manslaughter. Nielsen was sentenced to nine years in the Oregon State Penitentiary. With time off for good behavior, he got by with a mighty light rap.

10. The Blazing Ship Crashed and Exploded

The howling northwest wind and swirling fog ripped the coastline through most of the remaining days of July. It was as though the gods of the skies and seas were wreaking vengeance on this decadent earth where man ruthlessly kills his fellow man.

Venturing onto the raging ocean was next to impossible. The fog pressed in like a dank prison in which I chafed and brooded over the devilish urge that had prodded me into leaving the security of the newspaper and city life for this brutal, windy place where the sun vanished for days on end and shootings took place in broad daylight in the center of town.

I was ambling down the town's gravel sidewalk, head bowed against the wind and fog, when Ruth caught up with me. She sensed my somber mood and tugged me to a booth in the Spouting Horn Restaurant, where hot coffee partially buoyed my sagging spirits and Ruth's smile shot them top deck.

"If you'll drive me north of town a little way, I'll show you something that'll take your mind off your woes—if that bucket of bolts you call a car will run, that is," she taunted.

"What I'm going to show you is only accessible at low tide, which will be in a few minutes," she added, "so let's get motivatin'."

She paid for the coffee, and with her arm under mine, propelled me to the car. A new battery I'd installed effected the cure, and we headed north up the highway. A mile or so north of town she directed me to park alongside a sea-exposed cove. A forest-topped bluff to the north created a lee, which cut down the wind and thinned the fog along the cove's easterly shore, revealing a sea-battered jumble of rocks.

A nearby highway sign bore the legend: "Boiler Bay." Like most newcomers and tourists, I assumed it to be so named because of the crash and boil of Pacific combers that continually lash its rocky perimeter.

Ruth squared me away, pointing to a rusty ship's boiler nestling in a hollow in the rocks behind a breaker-bashed rock shelf. She informed me that the boiler, for which the cove was named, was once the steam-spawning heart of the 174-foot steam schooner *J. Marhoffer*, which smashed onto the rocks in flames in May, 1910.

She led me down a steep trail to the rugged shore, and as we scrambled over the rocks toward the boiler we discovered scattered among the boulders a clutter of rusted gears, shafts, cogs and various hunks of metal that had been the *Marhoffer's* steam engine. Clambering atop the twelve-foot-diameter boiler, we were astounded to find it sturdy and intact, despite its years of pounding by crashing breakers.

Discerning my interest, when we had finished beachcombing, Ruth had me drive to the home of pioneer resident, Tony Wisniewski, who, she told me, had been at the cove when the *Marhoffer* was wrecked.

"I was a young boy at the time," Tony said, "but I've recounted the tale many times and clearly recall what the captain and crew told us:

"In the early afternoon of May 19, 1910, the *Marhoffer*, in ballast out of San Francisco, was steaming northward off Cape Foulweather toward her Columbia River destination. Captain Gustave Peterson, on the bridge checking his position, looked up from his chart and mentioned to his wife, aboard as a passenger on this voyage, that the ship was logging good headway at a steady nine knots.

"The rythmic pulsation of the ship's triple-expansion steam engine lulled the chief engineer, off watch, into deep sleep in his cabin. In the engine room the first assistant engineer was laboring over a balky blowtorch that refused to light. Pumped up to high pressure, the torch suddenly exploded, hurling flaming gasoline through the engine room.

"Before the scorched assistant could grab a fire extinguisher, the engine room erupted into a roaring inferno. He rushed to the chief's cabin and jerked him awake. The chief took one look and bolted toward the bridge to notify the captain, but Captain Peterson was already rushing to investigate the black, acrid smoke swirling through deck vents and passageways.

"'Flood the engine room!' he roared.

"But the order came too late, for seacocks and pumps were now red-hot and useless. Yet the steam engine continued running, out of control, driving the blazing ship full ahead.

"'Head her for shore!' Captain Peterson shouted to the helmsman. The helmsman swung the ship toward the rocky, comber-lashed shore, then bolted from the wheelhouse to escape the smoke and flames now eating their way toward the bridge.

"'Abandon ship!' bellowed Peterson.

"Number one lifeboat was hastily swung out and lowered, but the suck of the plunging ship's hull rolled it under, spilling its three occupants into the sea. Number two, containing the rest of the ship's twenty-one crewmen, including Captain Peterson and his wife, was quickly lowered without mishap, and the floundering occupants of the capsized lifeboat were hauled aboard.

"The dazed survivors stared horrified as the doomed ship, trailing a giant plume of smoke and flame, crashed into the rocky shore, burned fiercely for several minutes, then was blasted apart by a mighty explosion that left only the bow and boiler intact.

"I was watching it all from the bluff top on Boiler Bay's easterly side," Tony told us.

"She was about two and a half miles offshore when she caught fire," he recalled, "I could see a small speck drift astern of her, and I figured it was the lifeboat with her people. Then she came charging in belching flames, sparks and smoke like a volcano.

"She piled onto the rocks with a helluva crunching crash, heeled way over to starboard, then lay there burning like a

Bow section was only part of hull remaining after the 174-foot steam schooner *J. Marhoffer* crashed onto rocks in flames a mile north of Depoe Bay, May 19, 1910. (Courtesy Lincoln County Historical Society)

Norman Hendrickson inspects boiler of the *J. Marhoffer*. The boiler remains intact at this writing and sparked naming of the coastal indentation in which it lies—Boiler Bay. (Photo by author)

blast furnace. All a sudden her tanks exploded and shot timbers, chunks of steel and flame clear up into the trees behind me, a quarter of a mile away. If I hadn't ducked behind a tree I probably wouldn't be here telling this."

Mrs. Andrew Wisniewski, Tony's pioneer mother, we learned, had observed the *Marhoffer's* plight from her Lincoln Beach home, two miles north. Seeing the lifeboat approaching the narrow strip of sandy beach at the mouth of Fogarty Creek, a mile north of Boiler Bay, she rushed to the surf edge there, snatched off her red sweater and waved it vigorously as a signal that a landing could be made at this point.

Interpreting the red sweater as a danger signal, the men in the boat swung south and rowed three miles to Whale Cove, where they landed safely on the sandy beach. All survived except the ship's cook, who died from burns and exposure.

Tales of lost treasure run rife with most shipwrecks, and the *Marhoffer* is no exception. According to Tony, a strong box containing a large amount of gold coins and several diamonds was lost in the wreck and never recovered.

At this writing the boiler lies intact on Boiler Bay's rocky shore—an enduring monument to the SS *J. Marhoffer*.

11. Sea Creatures—Weird, Wondrous and Phantasmic

The demented wind at last subsided sometime during the night in early August. When I awoke, the quiet was so complete it was almost eerie.

I rolled from my bunk and peered through the wheelhouse windows at a star-studded sky swept clear of fog. The stars in the sky's eastern quadrant were beginning to pale, and some high cirrus clouds glowed pink, then burst into flame as the dazzling edge of the sun cracked the Coast Range rim.

The storm gods had vented their wrath and withdrawn. Fair weather and calm seas blessed the Lincoln County coast through nearly all of August.

Like the first stirrings of animals following long hibernation, the harbor came to life. The fleet became a bustle of skippers and crewmen shipshaping and readying their gear and warming-up engines. Commercial fishing and charter vessels thrashed to sea in continuous procession, *Tradewinds* among them.

The sea lay calm as a gently waving sheet of silk, reflecting the sky in the living blue of a kingfisher's wing feathers. The sea, too, came to life in a fantastic air-sea show of nature's creatures.

The prolonged wind had churned nutrients from the bottom of the sea to its surface in upwellings, spurring wild feeding frenzies. Sea birds of all types had gone crazy, thousands upon thousands of them squawking, whirling and diving helter-skelter over and into the ocean as far as the eye could see.

Here and there the sea's surface was pocked with the heads of sleek hair seals and ton-size Steller sea lions bursting

Seals, like curious, playful pups, sometimes surface near vessels at sea. (From author's collection)

from the blue surface with salmon clamped crossways in their mouths. They played with their catches like a cat with a mouse, tossing the gleaming silver salmon in the air time after time and unerringly catching them in their mouths and shaking their heads furiously, then repeating the process until they'd tired of their play.

Then they would swallow their prey in a few head-thrusting gulps, bark a couple times, and dive for more victims.

The triangular dorsal fins of sharks slashed the sea's gently heaving surface in many sectors as these swift, vicious predators competed with other creatures in the berserk feeding fracas. Salmon hit the anglers' lines and were boated fast and furiously, as though the fish were eager to escape the rampaging enemies in their watery domain.

"Thar she blows!"

The anglers' shouts cut through the bedlam in high-pitched excitement. Close on our port beam a pair of whales, rolling in graceful unison, heaved their boxcar-size backs from the sea, geysered their warm, stinking spout spray

Fifty-foot humpback whale leaping from the sea. Cetologists theorize that whales hurl themselves from the sea to escape enemies, shake crab-like sea lice from their bodies, and show off before their mates. (Photo by author)

across our decks, arched their backs and submerged in a shallow dive.

Five minutes later they again rolled their barnacle-pocked backs from the ocean a short way to the south, spouted, thrust their immense twin-fluked tails high in the air and plummeted from sight in their deep-sounding dive. We identified them as humpback whales from the glimpse we got of the huge wing-like flippers they use for steering.

Humpbacks, which grow to a length of around fifty feet, are of the group known as baleen whales because, instead of teeth, as in the toothed-whale group, they are equipped with baleen, a wall of bristly slats that grow from the upper jaw and act as a strainer.

Baleens include the enormous blue whales, the largest living creatures on earth. In March, 1926, a blue whale was taken near the Shetland Islands, off Scotland, that was so huge it was measured and proved to be an astounding 109-feet, 4½ inches in length, and weighed an estimated 200 tons, establishing it as the largest in recorded whaling history. It's an anomaly of nature that these largest of all creatures feed mostly on plankton, one of the sea's tiniest organisms.

August sailed along fair and calm, and with the mild weather came a transition in the ocean. It gradually warmed and took on a sapphire-blue hue, clear as a mountain lake.

Old-timers opined that the tropical-like water of the Japanese Current had swept inshore from its normal flow, fifty to two hundred miles offshore. The change slowed the salmon runs but brought strange new creatures.

Their arrival was heralded overhead by majestic white albatrosses swooping and soaring on graceful wings reaching to twelve feet from tip to tip.

Masters of the art of riding air currents for hours on end, with scarcely a flap of their great wings, albatrosses live most of their lives far from land, drinking ocean water and sleeping on the sea's surface. A mysterious nature-endowed sense leads them to areas of the greatest numbers of the fish, squid and other small marine animals they mostly feed on; thus, here they were, many miles inshore from their normal habitat.

Along with a few salmon, we started catching large numbers of hake, a skinny, dull silver-gray fish up to three feet in length. We had learned that American fishermen considered them inedible and a nuisance, so we chucked them overboard.

Many years later, hake—renamed whiting—leaped to prominence as an edible fish and are presently harvested by the thousands of tons.

Pacific mackerel, too, frequently hit our lures. Streamlined and an iridescent metallic blue in color, it reaches nearly two feet in length and is a tasty food fish. Another edible stranger to us was the slate-black sable fish, which grows to over three feet in length and often strikes in schools that hit every hook.

Our most "shocking" catch was a three-foot flatfish, sporting black polka-dots on its broad light-gray back. When I grabbed it to remove the hook, it zapped me with a nasty electric shock, and I flung it to the deck.

Later I learned that it was an electric ray, which possesses

Left: Linda Neal and Erin Woodmark pose with sixty-five-pound ocean sunfish boated by fisherman off Depoe Bay. Ocean sunfish, which frequent Pacific Northwest waters, have been caught to lengths up to ten feet and eighteen-hundred pounds in weight. (Photo by author) Right: The author with eight-foot octopus caught on ocean floor off Depoe Bay. (Photo by Bev Kunz)

a large pair of electric organs on each side of the head capable of producing a strong electrical charge.

It must be touched at two points to get the full shock, which is strong enough to temporarily paralyze a man's arm or knock him down should he step on one lying partially buried in the sand.

Fishermen venturing farther offshore than normal in quest of salmon reported catching large numbers of a fish they didn't recognize; so they threw them back into the sea. These fish turned out to be albacore tuna, now prized as "chicken of the sea," an annual multi-million-dollar fishery.

Toughing it out for salmon farther inshore, we were amazed to find ourselves escorted now and then by squadrons of warm-water porpoises—beautiful creatures, jet-black on their upper bodies and sheet-white underneath.

For several minutes they'd leapfrog alongside and dart back and forth across the bow like kids at play. Then as if at a signal, they'd go skittering off through the waves to look for another plaything.

Occasionally we'd happen onto seals floating sound asleep on their backs in the warm water, flippers folded over their bellies like old men dozing in their easy chairs.

While we were trolling on one trip, a monstrous head

Jodi Jackson examines eight-foot elephant seal that beached itself and died near Depoe Bay. Elephant seals attain a length of sixteen feet, weight of over two tons. (Photo by author)

suddenly popped from the water alarmingly near us, and we found ourselves under the scary stare of a weird-looking brute with an elephant-like trunk. I later learned that it was an elephant seal, which is the largest of all seals and grows to sixteen feet in length, twelve feet in girth, and weighs up to five thousand pounds.

Several times we surged close to huge silver-gray cart-wheel-shaped fish lying on their barn-door-size sides on the surface, their puckered mouths gaping open and shut. They proved to be ocean sunfish, which lie on their sides on the surface feeding on microscopic organisms and attain a weight of a ton, another of nature's anomalies.

While heading offshore on another fishing trip, about a mile offshore from us, we spotted what appeared to be a raft with some living thing perched on one end. We chugged to within a few yards of it and gaped in awe at an immense marine turtle, which normally inhabits tropical seas.

I later found that it is the largest living species of leathery

Leatherback sea turtle alongside vessel off Depoe Bay. These largest of marine turtles attain a length of eight feet and weight of a ton and occasionally leave tropical waters to plod north through Pacific Northwest waters. (Photo by "Woody" Woodard)

marine turtle, which reach a length of eight feet and a ton in weight, and occasionally venture from tropical to northern waters.

Reports of giant sea serpents and monsters I am inclined to discount as stemming from optical illusions or the transfer of large amounts of alcoholic beverages from bottles to sighters' stomachs.

From a distance the serrated backs of surfacing whales resemble huge, undulating serpents as they alternately roll from the sea and submerge. A column of porpoises swimming single file appears the same. Even columns of birds flying close to the surface appear to undulate like a serpent as they rise and dip over the waves.

Many times at sea I've investigated "sea serpents" and "monsters," only to find them to be gnarled, oddly shaped logs and other drifting objects, appearing much like grisly monsters raising and lowering their craggy heads as they heave and roll in the swells.

Six-foot wolf eel captured by skin divers on ocean floor off Depoe Bay. (Photo by author)

Several times I've checked out mysterious "periscopes" bursting from the sea "for a look," then submerging. They all turned out to be deadheads—waterlogged logs floating vertically, alternately ramming from the sea and disappearing beneath the surface.

Depoe Bay fisherman, Bill Church, told about spotting a "monster" surging in his direction while he was fishing off the northern Washington coast. When it got close, it proved to be two sea lions supporting a bleeding, injured third sea lion between them as they swam inshore toward a rocky sea lion habitat.

Veteran commercial fisherman, Mauri Pesonen, endured a frightening experience while salmon fishing off Depoe Bay. He had just landed a salmon in the fishing cockpit aft when a huge, bull sea lion catapulted from the water in pursuit of the boated fish and crashed into the cockpit beside him. He barely scrambled clear, grabbed his rifle from the wheelhouse and shot the lion dead.

Try as he might, he was unable to muscle the beast from the cockpit, so was forced to haul in his gear and return to port. The sea lion was hoisted clear with a dock crane and tipped the scales at eighteen hundred pounds.

12. "Killer" Is the Cry

"Sharks! Dozens of 'em! All huge!" squawked a passenger, flapping his hand toward the north. I snatched my binoculars from the wheelhouse and trained them in the direction of his excited gesticulating.

A half mile north of where we were salmon fishing off Depoe Bay, forty, fifty, a hundred sweeping black fins boiled through the Pacific's blue surface like slashing sabers. White spray spouts punctuated the surface over a ten-acre area.

"Killer whales!" I shouted. "Probably chasing that pair of whales we saw heading south."

The fast-moving beasts were soon all around us—rolling, spouting, leaping, whacking their twin-fluked tails on the sea. Several times dead-center collisions with *Tradewinds* seemed imminent, but at the last moment they'd sheer one way or the other and slash past.

Finally the last of the fast-moving beasts plunged by and we watched them churn over the horizon southward. Though they missed us and our gear, they either scattered the salmon or paralyzed them with fright. The bite quit. We hauled in the gear and thrashed to port.

In the fish-house office that afternoon, with Ruth beside me and her sea creatures book before me, we had a rousing scuttlebutt session about killer whales with several Depoe Bay fishermen—and learned much.

Killers are by no means a rare species of whale. They roam the seven seas from pole to pole and are quite often seen along the Oregon coast in pods of four to a hundred or more. Often referred to technically as the Orca, the killer whale is spectacularly identifiable by its rounded, bulbous

69

Surfacing killer whale near charter vessel off Depoe Bay. (Photo by Tom Getty)

"Spy hopping" killer whale near charter vessel off Depoe Bay. Cetologists theorize that whales occasionally thrust their heads and upper bodies high above sea's surface to have a look around; this is dubbed "spy hopping." (From author's collection)

head, the long, curving dorsal fin that rears from its back to a height of up to six feet, and by its white eye stripes and strikingly marked body—sleek black on top and pronounced white underneath.

Males attain a length of thirty-one feet; females sixteen feet, and all are equipped with a lethal set of two-inch-diameter teeth weighing up to four pounds each.

Killers are considered the most predacious of all mammals. Few denizens of the sea can equal their up to thirty-knot speed and agility. They travel in "wolf packs" and gang up on the larger whales, ripping at their lips, mouths and tongues and slicing through their flippers and tails, and sometimes biting their victims in the stomach or the genital area in a frothing bloody struggle that the killers almost always win.

Charter skipper and former commercial fisherman, Jim Tate, told of watching killer whales attack a gray whale off the southern Oregon coast. "Time after time the big gray whale would come charging out of the sea with killers hanging onto each side. Hugh strips of flesh and blubber were hanging from its body, and the killers finally finished it off in a bloody frothed, free-for-all feast."

The killer whale's appetite is immense, and it seems to fear nothing, attacking giant squid, walruses, sea lions, elephant seals, dolphins, whales many times their size, and all manner of creatures. One of the beasts, only sixteen feet long, when killed by man—his worst enemy—was opened up and found to have eaten thirteen porpoises and fourteen seals, along with fish and even birds for hors-d'oeuvres.

Eskimos at Cape Prince of Wales swear they have seen a killer whale hurl a two-thousand-pound walrus completely out of the water. Killer whales have even threatened men and dogs standing on ice floes, by shattering the ice around them in combined assaults, according to arctic explorers.

An eye witness stated that he watched a pod of some twenty killer whales encircle a group of about a hundred dolphins, then gradually close the circle. Suddenly a whale plunged at a dolphin and killed it, while the other whales held the remaining dolphins within the circle until, one by one, the killers darted in, seized one of the victims and devoured it.

Jaws of killer whale showing lethal set of two-inch-diameter teeth weighing up to four pounds each. (From author's collection)

Forty-foot gray whale that drifted ashore at Sandy Cove, Depoe Bay, a few years ago, after apparently being attacked by killer whales. (Photo by author)

A few years ago, Pete Szalinski, skipper of the tuna clipper *Golden Gate*, reported that while cruising along the California coast he and his crewmen were amazed to find themselves suddenly being paced by four gray whales, two on each side close aboard.

"They had run to the ship like chicks to a mother hen," Szalinski said, "for in a great circle around us were killer whales obviously after the grays. The grays stayed with us until the killers frothed off after easier prey."

Dougal Robertson, skipper of the forty-three-foot schooner *Lucette*, told a harrowing tale of a killer whale attack that sank the vessel while on a three-thousand-mile voyage from the Galapagos Islands to the Marquesas Islands in the summer of 1971:

"About twenty killer whales of all sizes struck the hull with sledgehammer blows of incredible force," Robertson related. "I remembered that the killer whale in Miami's Sea-quarium weighed three tons and that trainers said they attack at about thirty knots. It felt like three of them rammed us at once, and the water started pouring in with torrential force. The *Lucette* sank in a few minutes."

Robertson, the four members of his family, and a friend were miraculously rescued. His experience was unusual, for ferocious as they are, killer whales rarely molest vessels unless they are wounded.

Crewmen on a commercial fishing vessel heading to sea from a California port a few years ago spotted a killer whale and began shooting at it. According to witnesses, the whale sounded and a few minutes later, as crewmen fled to the bow, it charged from the sea at the vessel and crashed onto the afterdeck, crushing it and part of the deckhouse and springing the hull planking. Crewmen were plucked from the bow by another vessel just before their craft sank.

Killer whales stick together in close-knit family units, now and then rubbing against each other and their calves in apparent affectionate gestures. Though vicious when attacking enemies and seeking food in their open-sea element, in captivity they are docile, intelligent and easily trained. They have rarely, if ever, been known to attack divers or their trainers. Indeed, they seem to acquire a real affection for their human keepers.

Best advice, if you are on the sea when killer whales show, is shoot 'em with a camera, not a gun, Better to have a photo of a whale in your album than be a dinner of a whale in its stomach.

13. Sunk

August, though fair and calm, was not without trouble. On one trip a couple miles west of Depoe Bay, we had been circling in schooled salmon, boating the beauties till our arms were sore.

The anglers had all the salmon they could use, so we brought in the gear and I swung the helm for a Depoe Bay heading. Then I heard a "pop" somewhere aft, and the helm spun free as a roulette wheel.

We hove to, and a check aft revealed a sheared rudder shaft. Rejecting the shame of signaling another vessel for a tow, I removed a short bilge board and lashed it to the boat hook with the handle levered against the stern post and—with a hastily instructed passenger at the throttle and clutch controls—I steered on a boat-hook-board and a prayer to and through the blessedly calm channel to the dock.

During another salmon trip, bilge water flung by the bottom of the flywheel started splattering its tell-tale tune inside the engine compartment. I grabbed the bilge pump, offering a silent prayer of thanks to the Astoria fisherman who'd suggested I get it, and soon great amounts of bilge water began gushing over the side. Then I assigned a passenger with pumping duty while we quickly brought in the gear.

Next, I put another passenger at the helm to steer toward Depoe Bay while I sought the source of the leak. No luck. (As it turned out, the Pacific was gushing in through an inaccessible steel-pipe-in-brass, through-hull fitting that ectrolysis had eaten away.) Other passengers relieved the

man at the pump, but they were slowly losing the battle of
the bilge.

I coaxed every ounce out of the Frisco Standard, and with
Tradewinds settling lower and lower in the water, we
panted through the channel, made what had to be the fast-
est docking and passenger disembarkation in history, and I
shoved off for the beach on the east side of the bay.

The flywheel was throwing such a deluge through a
sprung engine compartment hatch, standing at the steering
station was like being inside a washing machine; but the
Frisco Standard—bless its iron heart—kept chugging.

Blinded and half drowned by bilge water, I rammed
Tradewinds toward shore.

Just as the bow crunched onto the gravel beach, down she
went, the grounded bow pointing at the Coast Range summit, the stern under water. Ruth was on the beach when I
squished ashore, wiping bilge water from my eyes.

"You pick the darndest places to go swimming," she
quipped.

At low tide, fisherman friends helped pump *Tradewinds*
dry, and as the tide came in we moved her up on the beach
to highwater line, propped her on even keel, located the culprit electrolysis-disintegrated, through-hull fitting and
replaced it—brass to brass.

Right here I want to hoist a big, red electrolysis-warning
flag before fresh-water sailors planning to cruise their craft
in salt water. In fresh water there is little if any problem,
but in salt water the insidious destroyer called electrolysis
can cause dangerous damage.

It's an electric current activated by salt water, and it
flows through metal objects on the vessel. Unless preventive
measures are taken, it can eat into or through propeller
shafts, rudders, propeller blades, through-hull fittings and
all manner of metal installations.

As with the electrolysis-destroyed fitting that sank *Tradewinds*, steel fittings in contact with brass or bronze are
particularly vulnerable.

Zinc is the hero metal that prevents electrolysis by ab-
sorbing the electrolysis charge. It is manufactured in various
shapes and forms that can be secured to shafts, rudders,

propellers and other parts, and can be bolted to the bottom of the hull as "ground plates" wired to the engines.

While *Tradewinds* was on the beach the next few days, we replaced all questionable fittings, installed zincs in all vulnerable places, oil-flushed and cleaned the Frisco Standard, repaired the water-damaged ignition system, and at high tide one afternoon backed off the beach.

Ruth met me at the dock. "You need a diversion," she announced. "There's a real low tide early tomorrow morning, and I'll be able to take you to a mystery shipwreck. Game?" For her I'd have been game to swim the Pacific to Japan if she asked.

14. Mystery Shipwreck

The burst of a bright dawn the next day found us Olds-mobiling nine miles north to Siletz Bay. Ruth had me park near the mouth of Schooner Creek where it flows into Siletz Bay, which at this low-tide stage was more sand than water.

"There's the reason for Schooner Creek's name," she said, pointing a quarter mile or so west to where the wooden ribs and timbers of a ship reared from the bay's sandy, normally water-covered bottom. We slogged through the sand toward the old ship, Ruth in the lead. The navy pea jacket, blue jeans and rubber boots she was wearing did not prevent me from admiring her nicely rounded stern.

I pace-measured the unidentified old ship at over a hundred feet in length. Probed with my knife, her ancient barnacle-encrusted wooden frames, deck timbers and hull planking, secured with wooden dowel fastenings, proved to be remarkably sound and firm.

An incoming wave gave me the excuse to grab Ruth in a smooching hoist away from the encroaching water. When the wave receded, we trudged to the Olds and drove off.

Later, plowing through yellowed newspapers, magazines and other documents, I spliced together the thread of the possible past of the mysterious old sailing ship. . . .

Heavy seas and powerful tidal currents perform cataclysmic feats along the Oregon coast each winter. Previously exposed reefs and rocks are buried under tons of sand bulldozed from the ocean floor by crashing breakers during a single tide, and just as quickly tremendous quantities of sand are scoured from the beaches, exposing such things as ancient tree stumps, agate beds and fossilized sea creatures.

The old wreck was thus exposed in its sandy grave. Time and tide have erased all positive clues to her identity, leaving only theories from which it is almost impossible to determine where legend ends and authoritative fact begins.

If the ship's battered bones could talk they would possibly tell of the thud and crash of arrows and tomahawks. Indian legend handed down through the generations tells of a ship that, long before white men invaded Pacific shores, sailed into the bay, ran aground, and was attacked by the natives who killed everyone aboard, dumped the cargo of sacked meal and kept the sacks for clothing.

The hundred-foot schooner *Sunbeam*, which cleared San Francisco in the late 1880s and was never heard from again, has been suggested by some historians as the ship whose last voyage ended in disaster on the Siletz sands.

Other marine chroniclers suggest that either the 113-ton schooner *Uncle John*, which was lost off Cape Foulweather in March, 1876, or the schooner *Phoebe Fay*, which stranded north of Cape Foulweather in April, 1883, could have been carried onto the Siletz sands on southerly winds and currents.

Most evidence seems to support the belief that Siletz Bay's lost schooner was the 125-foot brig *Blanco*, which was built at North Bend, Oregon, in 1860-1861 and is reported to have capsized off the Siletz in 1864 and drifted into the bay. Strong evidence for this is revealed in a letter written in 1864 by Ben Simpson, Indian agent at the Siletz Indian Agency, to H. H. Luce of Coos Bay. It reads:

"A large brig named *Blanco*, from San Francisco, was wrecked a few days since at the mouth of the Siletz River. I have just returned from an examination of the vessel. She is a total wreck; her masts are gone, her deck broken in, her hull is split from deck to keel, and I fear her crew are all lost.

"I found some iron, round and flat, still in her hull, and also a lot of rope rigging. In addition to these I found the following articles in possession of the Indians: Two kegs of nails, six sheets of zinc, one oil coat, seven pairs of gaiters, two pairs of boots, one calico dress and a lot of rope and sailcloth."

Unless the shifting Siletz sands someday give up positive proof of the ancient ship's identity, the truth of her origin will probably remain a mystery forever.

15. Free Roams the Gray Whale

Dead ahead—barely a boat's length—forty tons of gray whale erupted through the Pacific's gently heaving surface as the huge mammal exploded from the depths in a cyclone of spray. For a split second the monster hung poised thirty or more feet above us, his great jaws gaping, his tremendous tail beating the ocean's surface.

I slammed the Frisco Standard astern and for a heart-stopping moment thought it was going to conk, but it caught and as we backed off, the whale crashed sideways into the sea with a tidal-wave whack.

September of this year had coasted in with clear, warm "Indian summer" weather. Just ten minutes earlier we had cleared the Depoe Bay channel on a salmon trip and had churned west along the path blazed by a bright sun. But after our near collision with the leviathon, we hove to and watched while it leaped clear of the sea a half dozen more times, then disappeared beneath the surface.

A few minutes later it showed farther south, its mate alongside, their spout spray puncturing the surface, followed by their broad gray-black backs rolling from the sea, then submerging in a series of shallow dives. Finally the behemoths thrust their ten-foot-wide, twin-fluked tails high and plunged to the depths.

These two huge mammals turned out to be the vanguard of the tremendous six-thousand-mile migration of Pacific gray whales that takes place along the Oregon coast each fall, winter and spring, as it has for centuries. I had heard about this great migration, but actually witnessing its start

Surfacing gray whale. Note fine spout spray blowing from twin slits (nostrils) atop its head as it exhales. Also note white barnacles mottling its back.

Whale tail. Whales propel themselves through the water with up-and-down thrusts of their huge twin-fluked tails. (From author's collection)

spurred me to dredge every scrap of information I could about gray whales from writings about them and from talking to fishermen and others with knowledge about them and their antics.

Through my following years at sea I bulwarked my whale knowledge by chasing and pacing the giant mammals at as close range as prudent. Though a few grays show up as early as September, the bulk of the pods do not appear until December and January. From then until March they surge southward in almost continuous procession, their backs, tails and spout spray visible close offshore almost any hour of the day.

Traveling in pods of two to ten or more, they scull their boxcar-size bodies through the sea at an average four-knot clip for a fifteen to twenty-hour day, taking three to four months for the long migratory haul. When pursued by ships or natural enemies, grays have been clocked at a ten-knot speed for an hour or more, and to attain sufficient speed to leap from the sea they can accelerate to thirty knots, according to authorities.

The huge grays propel themselves with up-and-down strokes of their powerful horizontal tails—unlike fish, which have vertical tails. They steer with their flippers, which project as much as fourteen feet from each side of their body. Alternately surfacing, spouting and sounding, they periodically heave their immense tails high in the air at the start of their deep-sounding dive, followed by a ten to fifteen-minute submerged stint.

Their southward migration originates in their summer feeding grounds in the Gulf of Alaska, the Bering Sea and the Arctic Ocean. Their winter feeding, mating and calving grounds are in the bays and lagoons along the western shore of Baja California and the eastern side of the Gulf of California. Scammons Lagoon, a 250-square-mile body of water, 350 miles south of San Diego, is their principal winter habitat.

The lagoon is named after the famous whaling shipmaster, Captain Charles Melville Scammon, who took command of the brig *Mary Helen* in 1852, prowled the lagoon as his favorite hunting ground, killed hundreds of whales there and became an authority on whales and their habits.

No one knows how long these gray-whale migrations have been taking place—probably for many eons. Spanish Sea captain Sebastion Viscaino, sailing up the Oregon coast in the vicinity of Cape Blanco, noted in his log for one day in 1603 that they had sighted huge numbers of whales. That was seventeen years before the Pilgrims landed in America.

An adventurous group recently tried to record the heartbeat of a gray whale off the west coast of Baja California, hopeful of learning something more about heartbeat in general. They failed to get accurate timed beats, but deduced that the gray's heart beats only five or six times a minute, compared to the Arctic white whale's twelve to fourteen times a minute. Heartbeat of tiny mice runs from three hundred to six hundred times a minute. Heartbeat slows down as animals become larger.

Gray whales prefer shallow water, often swimming in the surf. I have seen them actually, scraping their ponderous sides against breaker-bashed rocks during their close inshore journey along the Oregon coast. A while back, Depoe Bay resident, Lavelle Connell, reported seeing a gray whale surface directly under the bell buoy, a half mile west of the Depoe Bay channel entrance.

"I saw it submerge close to the buoy," she declared. "Then suddenly the buoy rose into the air, leaned way over, and crashed back into the sea, rocking crazily, its bell clanging like mad."

Fishermen aboard vessels anchored at night have told of being startled awake by harsh, scraping noises against their anchor cables, accompanied by pitching and veering of their vessels. They attribute the disturbances to whales.

It is thought by many that whales' scraping antics are for the purpose of removing barnacles and crab-like whale lice which dig deeply into battle-incurred sores and cuts. Occasionally one of the beasts will run itself aground, as was the case with a forty-foot gray dubbed "Smelly Nellie," which committed suicide on the beach at North Cove in outer Depoe Bay in April, 1951, to the olfactory consternation of the local populace.

During a recent trip off Depoe Bay, the grays were rolling and spouting on all sides of my vessel, and as one mammoth brute rolled close aboard and snorted his odorous spray across our decks, a passenger from New York voiced the question that is put to me constantly, "Aren't they apt to ram a boat and smash it to smithereens?" Except for wounded whales, the answer is "no."

I have watched from the deck as a giant gray drove up from the depths like a surfacing sub to explode from the sea not twenty feet from my vessel. It swelled its great nostrils (blow holes) to geyser a cloud of warm, stinking vapor over us, then sounded without giving us a second look.

Several times I have gaped horrified, braced for the crunch, as whales surfaced, heading dead center for our hull, only to watch them gracefully submerge at the last minute, swim under the hull without so much as a scrape, then surface on the other side.

As far as I know, not once has an unmolested whale attempted to attack my vessel or any others in this area. With wounded whales, or whales being attacked, it's different. In the heat of attack they could ram and damage or sink a small craft in their frantic twisting, turning, leaping attempts to shake off their tormentors.

Whalers capture the whales by firing a harpoon from a cannon mounted on the bow. The harpoon head is filled with a bursting charge of powder, and the explosion scatters shrapnel-like metal pieces through the whale's body, killing it instantly. Occasionally the harpoon head fails to detonate; and then the whaler has a wound-maddened mammal on the end of his harpoon cable.

A few years ago, when whaling for some species was legal in United States waters, friends of mine had a close call while whaling off the northern California coast, in a wooden converted World War II minesweeper. The gunner fired a harpoon into a big whale, but the head failed to detonate.

The crew watched helplessly as the monster charged off, burned out the winch brakes, ripped the heavy harpoon-tethered cable from the smoking winch to the bitter end, and snapped it like thread.

As the crew stared, the whale, trailing the long cable, began swimming in a mile-diameter circle around the whaler.

Deciding they could fire a second hastily readied harpoon into the whale, capture it and recover their gear, the men eased their vessel toward the circling behemoth.

Before they came within firing range, it suddenly broke off its circling course, charged straight at the whaler, smashed into the side of the hull with a splintering crash, turned aft under the keel, bent both shafts, propellers and rudders, and thrashed off.

Crewmen barely got water-tight doors dogged down in time to prevent sinking, and limped to San Francisco on one engine for emergency repairs.

Crippled whales have often been known to plunge to the depths, ripping a thousand fathoms of cable from the windlass and snapping it like trout line at the bitter end. On one occasion a blue whale, shot with a harpoon that failed to detonate, towed the whaling vessel at eight knots for seven hours before giving up.

Wounded sperm whales are the most dangerous of the beasts. They have a gigantic head, which they use as a ram, and they have been known to smash into and crush the hulls of five-hundred-ton vessels.

During their long migration journey of three to four months, gray whales feed on such things as plankton, squid and fish. In areas where crustaceans are abundant they bottom feed by bulldozing huge furrows across the ocean floor with their lower jaw and scooping up crabs, shrimp, clams and anything else in their path.

When they have a mouthful, they close their great jaws, and with piston-like thrusts from their huge tongues (that weigh as much as three thousand pounds) they squish water and sediment out through the strainer-like bony baleen that lines their mouths. Then they lick the remnants from the baleen, swallow the food into their four-chambered stomachs, and chow is down.

Like all mammals, the grays have lungs. They must surface to breathe every four to fifteen minutes through twin blow holes atop their heads. The spout spray that whale watchers see is vapor caused by warm air expelled from the whale's lungs into the colder sea air.

Like all baleen whales, the grays do not have teeth; they thrash their mighty tails, their only weapon, to ward off enemies. Their greatest enemy, until recently, was man.

In 1791, seven ships of the New England whaling fleet sailed around Cape Horn on the first whaling venture in Pacific coast waters. By chance they sailed smack into the gray whale migration, from which they reaped a rich harvest.

Their return to New England with a fortune in whale oil spurred increasing numbers of Atlantic whalers into beating around the Horn to Pacific coast waters. In 1847, the "golden year" of American whaling, more than five hundred of the six hundred New England whaling ships plied Pacific waters.

Toll among the grays was tremendous. The species was slaughtered almost to extinction, making whaling for them unprofitable during the latter part of the nineteenth century. With the cessation of whaling the gray population gradually increased, and in the 1920s and 1930s whaling for them was resumed. Again their numbers were seriously depleted.

U.S. Fish and Wildlife Service counts show that grays were down to less than two hundred in 1930, a far cry from the thirty thousand estimated by Captain Scammon to be in Pacific coast waters in the middle nineteenth century.

Alarmed whaling nations went into belated action. In 1937, the United States enacted a law prohibiting the killing of gray whales, and in 1938 they were given complete protection by international treaty, which forbids the killing or taking of grays except by oborigines who use them as a food staple. In 1970, the fifteen-nation International Whaling Commission recommended that the prohibition on commercial hunting of gray whales remain in effect indefinitely.

Results are encouraging. Counts from shore and the air have shown an increase of about eleven percent per year. The gray population is estimated to number up to eighteen thousand at this writing.

Federal agencies have gone even further to protect the world's dwindling whale population. In 1970, the Interior Department put eight species of whales on the endangered species list, and early in 1971 the Department of Commerce banned the killing of any and all whales by any fisherman operating from U.S. ports, thus virtually putting an end to the three hundred-year-old U.S. whaling industry. That same year the Mexican government declared Scammons Lagoon a sanctuary for all wildlife in and around the lagoon, including whales. Thus their winter habitat remains safe and there they feed and breed and give birth to their calves until early spring, when they again churn to sea to start their northward migration.

It is thrilling to watch them roll and spout as they migrate along the coast in their mysterious sea world and it is exciting to get a close look at one of them that has come ashore and died in the land world. But, here, caution must be used, as U.S. Army Lieutenant Phil Sheridan found out the hard way while he was stationed in Oregon country in pioneer days. . . .

Word reached him of a battle being waged by two rival Indian tribes over division of a monstrous and very dead whale that had come ashore on an Oregon beach. Galloping to the scene with some of his troops, the lieutenant swung from his saddle and strode sternly up to the whale, his drawn sword flashing.

Dazzled by the splendor of this cavalry officer, the Indians ceased their battling and listened in awed silence as the lieutenant explained how the division was to be made. To emphasize his point, he raised his sword high above his head and brought it swishing down to mark the division in the whale's belly.

A mighty outrush of gas hit him full in the face, and he passed out cold. Two of his troopers dragged him off a safe distance, and the Indians resumed their fighting—with the lieutenant a meek and groggy bystander.

16. Rum Runner

Butch Munson came rushing aboard *Tradewinds* one morning in mid-September. "C'mon, Stan," he bellowed in his brusque manner. "Wantcha to try something that'll put hair on your chest."

In those days if Depoe Bay had boasted sidewalks it could just as well have rolled them up after Labor Day. With the drop in tourist traffic I had few charters and none on this day, so I followed Butch up the steps to his rusty old car.

We rattled south down the highway a mile, careened west a quarter mile down a narrow, forest-edged road, with pine and cedar branches slapping new scratches on the sides of the jalopy, then jolted to a stop at the brink of a sixty-foot bluff overlooking cliff-surrounded Whale Cove, which is shaped like a horseshoe with the open end on the westerly side.

Butch grabbed a shovel from the trunk and led me down a trail hacked through dense coastal vegetation to a sandy beach flanking the cove's easterly shore. We trudged a couple hundred yards north along the beach to a barely perceptible trail tunneled through thick brush up the side of a steep ridge.

Crawling on all fours, we worked our way up the steep trail to the ridge top, wormed north a few hundred feet, and emerged onto a tiny promontory covered with brush and stunted, wind-sculpured pine trees. Through a hole in the vegetation, Butch pointed out the Pacific Ocean hurling its powerful breakers against the jagged-rock base of our promontory perch on the north.

Whale Cove, a mile south of Depoe Bay, where rumrunners unloaded illicit liquor during Prohibition. (From author's collection)

Then Butch wriggled a few feet south and parted the bushes to reveal Whale Cove below us, sea swells charging through its horseshoe-like opening, and marching in ranks across its sun-sparkled surface to curl and break in lacy foam on the sandy beach.

Swearing me to secrecy, Butch crawled to a thicket beneath the branches of a gnarled pine, gingerly probed the pine-needle-carpeted ground with his shovel, grunted, dropped the shovel and pulled out the top of a rotting burlap bag.

Reaching carefully, he drew into the shade-mottled light a moldy, brown bottle, wiped it off on his dungarees and showed me a barely legible sticker proclaiming the contents to be high-quality English scotch whiskey. Confiding that I was the first and only person he'd showed it to, he carefully covered the remaining booze cache, and we crawled to an open spot overlooking the cove. He popped out the cork with a straining, clenched-teeth pull and tipped the bottle to his mouth in a long, gurgling guzzle.

"G-r-r-e-a-t!" he choked, wiping off the bottle top with the back of his hand and shoving it at me.

The first swig blew off the top of my head and capsized my stomach. I spewed booze all over the bluff top. On the next try, my throat and stomach were paralyzed enough to handle it. While we sprawled there passing the bottle back and forth, Butch rattled off the story of the rumrunner booze.

He told me that Whale Cove's name sprang from the Indians finding an eighty-foot whale on the beach there in 1903—pointing out that whales still swim into the cove occasionally. During prohibition, he said, the nickname Bootlegger Bay was hung on the cove because of the Canadian rumrunners that would sneak into it at night, anchor, and use rowboats to ferry the illicit booze to the beach, where shore gangs would hoist it to the bluff top with a block and tackle slung from a tree. He pointed to a big spruce towering over the bluff above the beach.

The tree also did duty as a signal pole, he said. If the coast wasn't clear for the rumrunner to come into the cove because of cops or other suspicious persons lurking about, the shore gang would hang one lighted lantern on a limb as a warning to head out beyond the three-mile limit to international waters, where they were safe from boarding.

Two lights hung on branches, one above the other, signalled that all was clear to enter. Each rumrunner would bring in several hundred cases of mostly bourbon and scotch, twenty-four bottles to the case, all carefully packed in straw-lined burlap bags; plus a bunch of casks of alcohol and rum. The shore gang would load it onto trucks parked on the tree-obscured road above for peddling to booze pushers and speakeasys all over the country.

The last rumrunner to come in, Butch said, wiping a trickle of scotch from his chin, was six years ago in the winter of 1932. It was a sixty-five footer named the *Sea Island*, which sailed from a Canadian port with several hundred cases of bourbon and scotch and a lot of casks of alcohol and rum.

The Sea Island tried to come into the cove on an unusually stormy night, crashed into a rock (Butch waved the bottle toward a jagged fist of rock visible between breakers on the cove entrance's south side) and the rock tore a hole in the hull, which burst into flame.

The crew abandoned ship in their skiff, made it through the surf to the beach, and the shore gang helped them land. Butch took a long pull from the bottle, hiccuped and went on. . . . They watched the breakers hurl the blazing boat onto the beach, where the combers and flooded hull doused the fire.

We shot the bottle back and forth a few times, and Butch chuckled at the rumrunner wreck's happy ending—for him.

Most of the booze cargo was in good shape, and as the tide ebbed, the rumrunners started unloading it and burying it and hiding it in caves, but daybreak caught them before they'd finished.

A local resident saw what was going on, and the jig was up. The rumrunners vamoosed and people flocked to the place like seagulls to salmon guts. Butch was one of the first. People were staggering all over the place with booze stashed in their pockets and their pants and anything else they could stow it in, to lug to their cars or hide somewhere. But at least twenty cases remained ditched around somewhere when Sheriff McElwain broke up the party.

Butch now chucked the empty bottle over the bluff, snaked to his cache, brought out another jug, and between giggles, guzzles and burps told me that the biggest shocker of the affair came later and that I should go to the county courthouse and get the dope. About this time the world became a whirling kaleidoscope. To this day I can't remember how we got to his car and made it to Depoe Bay.

After Ruth had poured aspirin-laced orange juice and quantities of black coffee into me the next morning, she drove my suffering body and sledge-hammering head to the courthouse at Toledo. A pretty county clerk assistant's big, dark eyes and warm smile shot my sagging spirits up considerably. At my request she produced the *Sea Island* rumrunner file and handed me the added dividend of a personal scrapbook in which she kept clippings, statements, and other information on unusual cases, of which the *Sea Island* episode was top deck.

Ruth and I retired to an anteroom where she began reading me information on the affair, with growing interest, while I scribbled notes. It proved more exciting than a best-seller adventure novel. . . .

A murky sun was hauling itself over the forested rim of the coastal mountains east of Vancouver Island as three Canadian rumrunners—*Stanley Babcock, Charles Ryall* and *William Keer*—eased the *Sea Island* from their Victoria, British Columbia, dock, cleared the harbor and headed westward down Juan de Fuca Strait.

The date was February 1, 1932; their destination, Whale Cove, where they were to rendezvous with a coastwide gang of rumrunners to whom they would deliver the fortune in illicit alcohol—whiskey and rum they'd spent all the previous night stowing in the *Sea Island's* hold. Late that afternoon they churned past Swiftsure Bank Lightship, which guarded the entrance to Juan de Fuca Strait, and swung their pitching craft south, heading into gusty headwinds and choppy seas.

Holding well offshore to avoid interception by patrol craft of the United States Coast Guard, they slugged their way slowly down the coast, raked by cresting seas and gale-force winds. Finally, just before darkness enveloped their plunging craft on Sunday night, February 7, the exhausted rumrunners made out Cape Foulweather's jutting promontory, which they knew was just south of Whale Cove.

They swung east and—staring through binoculars into the roiling murk ahead—at last made out the flickering yellow lights of the two lanterns the shore gang had hung on the "signal tree" on Whale Cove's easterly side. As they beat their way to the brink of the cove's breaker-lashed entrance, two of the rumrunners yelled a warning to the skipper that he was too far south and headed for the rock in the south side of the entrance.

While the skipper was shouting at them to mind their own blankety-blank business—he knew what he was doing . . . . *Crash!* A roaring comber slammed the embattled vessel against the rock, holing the hull and starting a fire in the engine room. They were barely able to get the skiff clear in the thrashing turmoil and make it to the beach.

When the gang was spotted ditching the booze next morning, most of them scattered and hid out till the heat was off. The three men from the *Sea Island* sped north up the coast highway in a stolen auto provided by the shore gang. At Hebo, forty miles north, bad luck struck again.

The car hurtled off the highway and overturned. None was injured and they boarded a bus for Portland, a hundred miles inland.

Later a state police officer, investigating the wrecked automobile, noticed that its license plates had been switched. Learning that its occupants had boarded the Portland-bound bus, he phoned Captain Gurdane of the state police at Portland.

Gurdane arrived at the bus depot just after the bus had pulled in and arrested the three Canadians as they were hopping a cab. They admitted being from Vancouver, British Columbia, and were held at Portland police headquarters for immigration authorities.

Meantime, Sheriff McElwain and his men loaded the contraband liquor onto trucks, hauled it to Toledo, and stowed it in a storeroom in the Lincoln County jail to be held as evidence. On the wrecked rumrunner they discovered evidence linking the three Canadians to the affair. Questioned in Portland, the Canadians admitted their guilt and were jailed to await trial.

But the most fantastic phase of the affair was yet to come. Shortly after midnight on Sunday, March 20, 1932, two trucks, a sedan and a coupe pulled up in front of the Lincoln County jail at Toledo. Two men in the coupe, armed with machine guns, stood guard while the seven men in the other vehicles hustled a portable cutting torch from one of the trucks, cut through three steel jail doors and a lock on the storeroom door, and loaded the liquor being held as evidence onto the trucks.

When the heist was completed, the trucks, convoyed by the sedan, sped off toward Portland. The armed coupe and its occupants, presumed to be the big bosses of the gang, were never found.

Discovering the jail hijack later that morning, sheriffs and state police fanned out over the highways but came within a squeak of being completely foiled by the hijackers. A final bad break finished the fantastic event.

Near Grand Ronde, thirty-five miles east of the coast, the larger of the two trucks ran low on fuel and both trucks were forced to stop while fuel was transfered from one to the other. Officers drove up while this was going on and arrested the four men manning the trucks—Nels Krueger, George Fisher, Elbert Johnson and Arthur Adams.

Two of the officers, dressed in plain clothes, drove on with the trucks as decoys. A few minutes later, spotting the convoy sedan returning in search of the trucks, they quickly parked and when the sedan stopped alongside they leveled their guns at its occupants.

With hands held high, Burt Chapin, Sydney Carrick, Paul Remaley and the three Canadians, who'd been sprung on bail, gave up without a struggle. Several guns and saps found in their vehicles were confiscated, along with the vehicles and liquor.

All were sentenced to fines and penitentiary terms on charges ranging from destruction of public property and theft of government evidence to transporting and having in possession, while armed, alcohol and moonshine whiskey in violation of the National Prohibition Act.

When Prohibition was repealed on December 5, 1933, pending indictments against the prisoners were dismissed.

17. Juggernauts

Equinox! After mid-September that word was on the tongue of every fisherman and vessel operator.

In spite of continuing windless days topped with a great dazzling orb of sun beaming its rays on a sparkling, calm ocean, fishermen were reluctant to sail and spent hours staring seaward for signs of disturbance.

The culprit cause of mass uneasiness was the dreaded specter of the autumnal equinox looming like a monstrous sea demon over sailors throughout the seven seas, waiting to swat its victims to destruction.

The awesome elements usually, though not always, annually produce two man-humbling equinoctial displays of might. The vernal or spring equinox occurs about March twenty-first; the autumnal equinox about September twenty-first. They take place when the sun crosses the celestial equator, at which time the days and nights are of equal length.

Sometimes the equinoctial weather demons come screeching from the heavens in devastating winds that team up with the sea devils to churn the ocean to a roiling hell's broth. Other times the ocean will be oily calm under an ice-clear sky when, without warning, giant swells come rolling in from the vast reaches of the ocean, where they've been whipped up by violent storms and other cataclysmic disturbances hundreds, sometimes thousands of miles away.

Along the Pacific Northwest coast, the giant ocean swells are usually not generated by local storms but are churned into tumultous action by distant typhoons, ocean-floor volcanoes, earthquakes, massive undersea avalanches and other titanic earth-sea convulsions, which sometimes not only churn up the entire North Pacific but rake the Pacific's sixty-four million square miles from Alaska to the Antarctic.

A couple of days after the 1938 autumnal equinox, which sailed in and out of the Depoe Bay area with silky calm sea and weather, several fishermen and I were elbow-hunched over the concrete rail on the west side of the Depoe Bay highway bridge, staring seaward for signs of disturbance, when wham!—my backbone rammed through my chest, exploding my breath out in a tongue-curling whoosh.

When I'd realigned my spine, replaced my tongue and gulped resuscitating sea air into my collapsed lungs, I staggered sideways and gaped at a grinning, red-faced baboon drawing a helm-size paw from my shattered back.

"Ahoy, cousin," guffawed the hulking, big-bellied baboon. "Me 'n the wife and m' friends here—he swept his big paw toward two comely, quiet, early-thirtiesh women and a pleasant though embarrassed-appearing man—are the ones got you chartered this morning. Let's get with it!"

The other man in the group, a reedy, wiry-appearing individual with sparse sandy hair and a firm handclasp, introduced himself as Frank "the Lank" Harding and presented the two ladies: his wife, Jan, a plumpish, dark-eyed brunette, whose warm, dimpled smile quickly negated the first impression of stout sternness; and Blowhard's wife, Penny Landis, a slender redhead with striking green eyes that flashed wisdom, understanding and fun.

Through a forced smile I explained to them about the hazards of the equinox, necessitating our sea scanning for danger signs. As I talked, Blowhard's lower jaw jutted out farther and farther, like a Ubangi witch doctor's.

Then, suddenly, the sea pounced. Seemingly from out of nowhere a rush of six or seven giant swells reared their tons of green water thirty or more feet skyward on the reefs a half mile northwest and southwest of the channel entrance, curled their jagged claws and broke in a thunderous roar like a battleship broadside.

Then the sea subsided to eerily-deceptive windless calm. The Pacific's heavy artillery had boomed its warning of the massive attack to strike later, then retreated.

With no widespread electronic warning systems such as used today, we puny humans were totally ignorant of the approach of the Pacific's powerful attack force—rank upon rank of massive swells, a half mile or more between racing crests—marching eastward across the North Pacific from the devastating typhoon that had spawned them several days earlier during the equinox on the other side of the Pacific off the coast of Japan, nearly five thousand miles to the west.

During the lull, Blowhard bored in again. "S'matter, cousin," he snarled, "you chicken?" Those waves were just freaks. Hell, I've been in swimming pools rougher'n that ocean is now."

I tried to explain that, according to the old-timers, the crashing giants we'd gaped at on the reefs were just a sample of what was to come and served warning to stay in protected water.

"Hawgwash!" Blowhard boomed. "We drove more'n a hundred miles to come here an go fishin', and you damn well better take us, cousin!"

"Look, mister," I bridled, riveting him with the most crucifying stare I could muster. "I am not your cousin. I am no relation to you. I have never met you before. My name is Allyn, Stan Allyn. Call me Stan. If it looks like it's going to stay safe, we sail. If not—tough!"

Penny sidled over to me. "Don't worry about Ratchet Jaw," she whispered, cocking her burnished-copper head toward her blustering husband. "You're the skipper; we'll do what you say."

I should have pulled a heave to and canceled the trip on the spot, but a half hour's continuing calm and the big goon's goading influenced my against-the-grain decision to sail.

No sooner had Grumble Gut planted his big butt aboard than he began razzing the others in the group about how seasick they were going to get and bragging about how he'd sailed the seven seas through history's fiercest typhoons and tidal waves, fearlessly and without seasickness.

Gentle waves lapping the channel-edge rocks as we surged seaward beckoned us on, negating the head shakes of veteran fishermen sensing our sailing to equinoctial disaster.

About four miles west of the channel entrance, I notched the Frisco Standard down to trolling speed and began laying out the gear.

While Blowhard was bragging about the biggest salmon in the sea he was going to battle to gaff, Jan called my attention to the western horizon. I stared to the west at a green mountain sweeping toward us, its ragged crest blotting out the lower half of a row of billowing cumulus clouds ranged along the horizon.

Bow pointed into it, *Tradewinds*, as in slow motion climbed its quarter-mile-long frontal slope. On the hissing crest the little craft seemed to hang poised for a time, and we had the sensation of balancing on a lofty ridge while we peered into the dark green abyss of the following trough. Then we slithered down the monster swell's foam-ribboned back side to the trough, where *Tradewinds* paused as though gathering her muscles for the ascent to the next towering crest.

Looking shoreward, I was shocked to note that the intervening wave crests blocked out all view of even the summits of the highest Coast Range Mountains.

Tradewinds roller-coastered over a series of successively lessening seas, which gradually smoothed to near normal. The air remained cathedral calm. During quiet periods between series of giant swells, we chased scatterings of birds and trolled a few circles, but the salmon were smarter than us. In the face of the Pacific's approaching onslaught, they had sounded or gone somewhere else. Nary a strike did we get.

After checking the Frisco Standard's heart-beat, I stepped from the wheelhouse to seek the source of the moaning coming from the afterdeck. Sprawled with his sternsheets on the deck and his back against the bulwark was Blowhard, his double chin sagging on his slipped chest, his head lolling back and forth with the roll. The yellowish-green pallor and sheen of perspiration on his forehead clued his intestinal status.

Looking up at me through bleary eyes under halfmasted lids, he burbled: "For Gawd's sake, take us in, Allyn. You shouldn't a brought us out in the first place in a sea like this. Whaddaya tryin' to do, drown us all? He then puked forth a stream remarkable in its variegated content and volume; then flopped on his back and lay groaning in the scuppers.

Blowhard became Beghard. With his pleadings to take him to port rattling my eardrums, and worry of what these mountainous seas must be doing to Depoe Bay's channel entrance wrenching my guts, I secured the gear and headed *Tradewinds* east.

Racing ahead on the creaming crests, and seeming to backslide into the following trough chasms, we worried toward the Depoe Bay sea buoy. The increasing scarcity of flat spots grabbed my jittery awareness.

The tormented surface built to an almost continuous procession of racing giants that leaped to steeper crests as we approached the plunging sea buoy—visible only when heaved to its roiling zenith on the foaming wave tops. While Beghard wallowed in the sea-sloshed scuppers aft, the other three passengers stood quietly behind me in the wheelhouse.

"Hang on!" I yelled. A curling white following crest flung *Tradewind's* stern at the sky, lashing me with the terrifying thought that we were going to be hurled pitchpoling end over end down the seething wave face.

I rammed the Frisco Standard full astern and, slithering slantways down the massive wave front, like a surfer riding a giant comber, the blessed little gillnetter recovered, slued violently around to port, and I got her headed slow-bell into the mammoth seas, high as six-story buildings.

"Most any vessel will bring you through safely if you keep it in deep water." The veteran fishermen's advice banged at my brain.

We slogged slowly west.

While pitching over the sky-high crests we gaped shoreward at the awesome spectacle of the attacking giants slamming the rocky shoreline with repeated sledgehammer assaults, crashing and leaping in a roaring, white-frothed mad dance, flinging their spray a hundred feet above the sixty-foot, ocean-edge bluff tops.

I informed my passengers that we'd have to ride it out in the deep through the heaving, windless night and go in on slack flood tide next morning—if the sea had moderated enough to run the channel safely.

Pacific juggernauts slam their might against the rocky shore near Depoe Bay. (Photo by author)

Crewmen aboard Coast Guard motor lifeboat preparing to heave a line to the fifty-foot yacht *Enid III*, which had been hurled onto the rocky shore at the Depoe Bay channel entrance by storm-lashed breakers while attempting to seek refuge in Depoe Bay harbor. (Photo by author)

"I'll keep the coffee going," volunteered Penny, backed up by Jan's offer to whomp up what chow was available and Frank's cheerful insistence on spelling me at steering, standing lookout watches, or helping in any other way he could. Beghard was a mass of blubber wallowing comatose in the scuppers.

The hours sluffed into a melange of clawing up the gargantuan wave summits and swooping to the troughs, like a sea-mauled yo-yo. Finally, the lowering sun abruptly disappeared behind a billowing crest, reappeared briefly, then scuttled itself beyond the ragged, western horizon.

Like films developing, the stars began to emerge to prick the great vault of the darkening heavens. The hiss of the rushing seas and the throb of the Frisco Standard rode the tumultuous night as we clawed and lunged back and forth on alternate westerly and easterly headings, five to six miles offshore.

Through that endless night, my three able-bodied passengers spelled each other at plying me with coffee, standing lookout and dozing.

An eternity slogged by and at last the shadows began to pale. A lightening gradually melted through the darkness, and the cobalt shadows of dawn whirled around the heaving sea, then blazed into dazzling shimmer as the sun cracked the Coast Range rim in the east.

Mesmerized, we blinked at the dawn-sparkled swells, squinted toward the east, and yelled a hoarse chorus at the sight of moderated seas breaking against the shore in nearly normal force. I swung *Tradewinds* to an easterly heading, squeezed the maximum six knots out of the Frisco Standard, and we thrashed toward Depoe Bay.

A half mile off the channel entrance, I notched the throttle down while we zigzagged through a "Sargasso Sea" of planks, logs, hatch covers, floating docks and all manner of flotsam—grim clues to the devastation the brawling seas had wrought during their titanic rampage through the rocky-gorge channel into the tiny harbor.

During a flat spot between the moderating rushes, we surged through the channel entrance, scudded to the harbor mouth—and backed down full.

Depoe Bay looked like this after being ravaged by heavy seas before Army Engineers deepened the harbor and channel and built protective breakwater and seawall in 1950. (From author's collection)

The place was a nightmare shambles. Nearly every dock and vessel had been ripped loose from its moorings. Some had been mauled to wreckage. Several vessels were canted at crazy angles along the shore. Masts and top hamper stabbed from the bay's turbid waters where several had sunk.

A macrame of mooring lines spiderwebbed the little harbor, attesting to fishermen's desperate attempts to save their embattled vessels by mooring to harbor-edge trees, stumps, rocks and anything else to which they could secure a line. We finally tied precariously to some listing dock piling, and a group of fishermen on shore worked a two-by-twelve out to us as a makeshift gangplank.

Ruth bounded aboard and bear-hugged the hell out of me, while fishermen assisted my passengers to the hallowed, solid earth. Frank's vise-grip handshake was sheered away by Jan's and Penny's storm of smooches in an ardent show of gratitude for our safe return.

Ruth arm-yoked me away in mid-smooch and towed me to her apartment. My last awareness was of her easing me onto her sofa and the delicious feel of her smooth cheek against my three-day stubble.

18. Beach Bounty

The gods of the seas were appeased. Nature's awesome forces had wrought vengeance for man's challenges and retreated. As September coasted into October, the ocean along the Pacific Northwest coast, as if in atonement, subsided to gently undulating seas kissed by a moderate westerly wind.

"Westerly! Beachcomber wind!" exclaimed Ruth, plunking down her cup in a shower of spilled coffee. She and I were in a Spouting Horn Inn booth on a bright October morning, recounting the recent sea drubbing.

She explained that storms along Oriental shores tear glass fishing floats from their nets and rip other gear and flotsam from wrecked ships and what-not, and sweep them into the Japanese Current, which carries them northeastward in a giant Alaska-skirting loop to a southerly drift along the west coast of the United States.

"West winds blow all kinds of things out of the Pacific Northwest swing of the Japanese Current and shove them ashore," she expounded. "C'mon, I'll take you to a peachy beachcombing spot."

She bounded to her sneaker-clad feet, tugged me upright and hustled me outside to my car. A short drive north landed us at a tree-tunnel trail through cedar and jackpine. Then abruptly we burst onto a secluded cove flanked by a sandy beach.

Ruth yelped and streaked seaward, her golden hair streaming aft in a shimmering flood. At the ocean edge she snatched up a green, bowling-ball-size glass fishing float.

While she was caching it behind a log, I pounced on two more barnacle-encrusted floats.

That triggered us and we went rioting up the beach, tearing through piles of logs, boxes, boards, hunks of boat wreckage, tangles of flotsam and mounds of seaweed and kelp torn from the seabed by the recent heavy seas.

When our foray was over, we squatted panting in the sand by our bounty, which boasted thirty-three multicolored baseball to basketball-sized glass floats and a stainless-steel buoy the size and shape of a large watermelon. Chattering like seagulls scavenging salmon roe, we lugged them to my car in gunnysacks we'd brought, headed to her cottage, spread them out on the lawn, and gloated.

Our prizes from the sea primed my curiosity, and the next few days I tracked down information about the Japanese Current and its bounties. . . .

Discovery of a fortune in cargo flotsam from a wrecked ship or a treasure in coins and jewels in a pirate's chest is the hope of every beachcomber. While chances of making such a discovery are remote, valuable things do now and then turn up on the beaches.

One beachcomber trudging along an isolated beach a few years back happened upon an odorous mass that sparked thoughts of the beachcomber's dream discovery—ambergris, a morbid secretion from the intestines of the sperm whale, highly valuable as a base in making expensive perfumes.

The beachcomber trekked to his home, returned to his fumy find with a washtub and a clothespin for his schnoz, and hauled the stuff to the nearest chemist, who proclaimed that it *was* ambergris—worth sixty-six thousand dollars.

Frequent reports were circulated during and following World War II of the finding by beach walkers of waterproof cases containing watches, jewelry and all manner of merchandise that had drifted ashore from torpedoed merchant ships.

An experiment was conducted in 1963 by a trading company in Japan to determine the routes and time taken by Japanese current-borne flotsam. The firm released 120 "friendship buoys," each containing a letter with release date and place, also a certificate for a free watch. The first buoy found on the Oregon coast drifted ashore near the northern coast town of Nehalem in 1966, following 4,400-mile drift from Japan at an average 4.4 miles per day.

The Japanese Current starts its powerful flow off the east coast of Taiwan, where it is called Kuroshio (black stream). It swirls northeastward along the Japanese islands at a rate varying from one to five knots, then skirts the Aleutians in its gigantic sweep, finally curving southward along the coast of Alaska, British Columbia and the Pacific Northwest, where it merges with the California Current.

Off Mexico it starts a westerly push known as the North Equatorial Current, which surges across the Pacific to Oriental waters, where the Japanese Current takes over and repeats the massive cycle.

On the north-bound Oriental segment, its clear, blue tropical waters average one hundred miles in width and three thousand feet in depth. On its southerly push off the west coast of the United States it widens to an average three hundred miles but recedes to a depth averaging six hundred feet. Travel time in the trans-Pacific drift is erratic. It may take only a year for flotsam to cross from Oriental waters to Pacific Northwest shores, or it may take decades. Once it reaches shore it becomes fair game for beachcombers.

Strewn along Pacific Northwest beaches, following westerly winds, are all manner of objects—bottles, boxes, boards, bamboo, kegs, ropes, fishing gear, portions of wrecked vessels, even Japanese mines, which were cast ashore by the score for several years after the end of World War II.

Most prized of the sea's gifts are the amber, green, blue and purple glass balls or net floats lost by fishermen on the other side of the ocean. These range from golf-ball size to more than sixty inches in circumference.

While most of the floats bear Japanese markings, occasionally they are inscribed with the hammer and sickle, bearing witness to their Russian origin. Rare metal specimens have been found carrying Chinese inscriptions. Even rarer than spherical floats are rolling-pin-shaped floats, and during recent years many plastic and metal fishing buoys have drifted ashore.

There is definite correlation between typhoons and tidal waves in Oriental waters and spectacular finds along the

Left: Japanese glass float wearing beard of barnacles, attesting to many months of drifting in Pacific's Japanese Current from Oriental waters to the Pacific Northwest, where unidentified men spotted and retrieved it while on charter-fishing trip off Depoe Bay. Right: Mrs. Leroy Grant poses on driftwood with ceramic-like urn she found on beach at Lincoln Beach, just north of Depoe Bay. Oriental characters on urn indicated it had drifted across Pacific in Japanese Current. (Photos by author)

Mrs. Ray Wilson poses on beach near her Lincoln City home with thirty Oriental glass fishing floats she found there. Carried across the Pacific in the Japanese Current, they range from the size of an orange to bigger than basketballs. (Photo by author)

Oregon coast several months later. Flotsam travels in a zone fifty to two hundred miles off the Oregon coast until westerly winds or freak currents carry it shoreward.

Nature even signals advance notice of arrival of Oriental floats and flotsam with a small jellyfish called Velella, commonly known as Portuguese man-of-war, which has a blue base about two inches across on which it floats, and a triangular sail-like projection. Hordes of Velella often drift ashore a day or so ahead of Oriental flotsam.

Occasionally Japanese light globes are found on the beaches, such as the hundred-volt, thousand-watt bulb discovered on Salishan Spit, a few miles north of Depoe Bay, by Mrs. Kenneth Casey of Lincoln City, Oregon, in January, 1972. Screwed into a light socket, it functioned perfectly despite its barnacle-encrusted exterior.

Message-bearing bottles are periodically pounced on by beachcombers. Notable among them are a barnacled bottle picked up by Otto Kruger on the beach near his Otter Rock home just south of Depoe Bay in 1939. A moldy note inside stated that it had been cast adrift from the shore of Japan in 1918—twenty-one years earlier.

Another message found in a bottle a few miles south of Depoe Bay in 1969 by Debbie Holms of Waldport, Oregon, proclaimed that W.A. Nassey of Suffolk, England, had cast it into the sea from the merchant ship *Orcades*, fifteen hundred miles off Yokohama, January 16, 1960.

A bottled, English-authored note was found on the beach at Neskowin, Oregon, twenty-five miles north of Depoe Bay, in 1969, by Mr. and Mrs. Ralph Hazelton of Lincoln City. Written by Gerald Holt of Leicester, England, it stated that he had cast it into the Pacific five hundred miles off Tokyo from the merchant ship *Stanwear*, while tramping from Cuba to Japan and India in the summer of 1964.

By unusual coincidence, in March, 1972, Hazelton received a letter from Joyce Patterson, a Wake Island resident, stating that she had found a bottle on a Wake Island beach containing a message signed by him. It proved to be one of several message-bearing bottles he cast into the Pacific between 1920 and 1969 while he was a Merchant Marine radio officer.

Prize finds now and then are Oriental-fired pottery urns.

Experts have proved them to be common carriers of oil, water, grain and booze used on ancient Oriental fishing vessels.

Many strange objects are given up by the sea. Early one morning a friend and I were amazed to come upon a dead camel lying at the edge of the surf. Other beachcombers have discovered such things as elephant seals, porpoise, barracuda, handsaw fish, weird ten-armed squid, octopuses, sharks and various species of whales.

Lincoln City beachcomber, Bill Watson, stumbled upon a fifty-thousand-year-old mastodon molar protruding from the sand at nearby Gleneden Beach; and Ernest Marler, of adjoining Lincoln Beach, was astounded to discover an ancient Oriental urn lying beside an aged, worm-riddled mahogany ship's mast. Flabbergasted was Norman Jacobson's reaction when in January, 1973, he came upon a boxcar complete with its cargo of sacked gluten flour on the beach at Seal Rock, twenty-five miles south of Depoe Bay.

The strangest creature discovered on Depoe Bay area beaches was the three-thousand-pound sea monster dubbed Old Hairy, which washed ashore near the mouth of the D River, twelve miles north of Depoe Bay, in April, 1950. Equipped with feathers and hair and an appendage measuring sixteen feet in length, it made world-wide headlines, piqued the curiosity of oceanographic scientists the world over, and defies identification to this day.

Probably the most astounding object borne to Pacific Northwest waters in the Japanese Current was the eighty-five-foot Japanese fishing vessel which drifted from the coast of Japan to near grounding on the Washington coast with its grisly cargo—the bleached bones and withered bodies of all twelve dead crewmen, a tale of suffering and death that morbidly merits a separate chapter. . . .

19. Death Held the Helm

A misty pall hung over the Pacific's heaving, slate-gray surface as the merchant ship *Margaret Dollar* steamed along the northern Washington coast toward Juan de Fuca Strait on October 31, 1927.

On the freighter's bridge, Captain H.T. Payne ordered extra lookouts posted as a precaution against collision danger in the heavily traveled shipping lanes leading to and from the strait, gateway to Puget Sound, British Columbia and the inside passage to Alaska.

Fifteen miles south of Umatilla Reef Lightship, a lookout reported a small vessel off the starboard bow. Captain Payne focused his binoculars on what he expected to be one of the many American fishing vessels that frequently troll that area. Abruptly he ordered a course change toward the vessel—the strangest craft he had ever seen in these waters.

Hove to alongside a few minutes later, the crew stared down at stark dilapidation. The strange vessel's narrow hull reached forward to an overhanging sampan-type bow. A wooden taff rail around the stern was supported by carved stanchions, like those of old-time sailing ships.

Shredded canvas hung from two battered masts. Yellowed, once-white paint peeled from the rust-streaked deckhouse and hull. As the eerie craft rolled in the ground swell, the men could see a solid crust of barnacles below the waterline and seaweed streamers several feet long.

The deck was a litter of wreckage, amid which human bones, bleached and clean-picked, gleamed white in the

Eighty-five-foot Japanese fishing vessel *Ryo Yei Maru* in Puget Sound, where she was towed after being found adrift off the northern Washington coast by the merchant ship *Margaret Dollar*, October 31, 1927. A four-inch coating of barnacles encrusted her hull, attesting to her long drift across the Pacific after becoming disabled off Japan December 12, 1926. Only human bones and two withered bodies were found aboard, along with a diary kept by various crewmen relating tragic events until the last man died.

murky light. Faded black lettering on the transom bore the wording: RYO YEI MARU, Misaki.

Captain Payne ordered a boat lowered, and a crew soon made fast alongside the wallowing mystery craft. As the men cautiously hauled themselves over the bulwark, the only sound that greeted them was the clatter of loose gear banging in the rigging as the vessel rolled. Somewhere below, a door rasped to and fro on rusty hinges.

The men picked their way forward; wrenched the hatches ajar; peered into the holds. Nothing there. They crept into the pilot house and found only an unmanned helm and musty litter.

Then they pried open the engine-room hatch. A rusty,

partially dismantled two-cylinder gasoline engine was visible in the gloom. Oily bilge water sloshed from side to side, splashing over the engine and scattered parts and tools on the floorboards alongside.

Tenseness gripped the men as they reached the hatch leading to the crew's quarters. When they forced it open, an escaping wave of stinking, foul air all but turned their stomachs. Covering their nostrils with handkerchiefs, they inched down the ladder and found themselves in the dank murkiness of a tiny galley. In corroded kettles on a rusty stove they saw human bones.

Creeping aft, they discovered tiers of wooden bunks, all empty—save two. There, huddled side by side, were the withered bodies of two dead Japanese.

The boarding party fled to their boat, returned to the freighter and reported their ghastly findings.

Captain Payne, following instructions radioed from Seattle, ordered a towing hawser secured to the derelict, and the ship resumed its course. For the first time in nearly eleven months the eighty-five foot, hundred-ton Japanese fishing vessel, *Ryo Yei Maru*, was under way.

That night the *Margaret Dollar* arrived at Port Townsend, Washington, with her strange charge. Officials immediately boarded the derelict to search for some clue to the mystery.

"There is mute evidence of the clean-licked human bones, which clearly points to cannibalism," declared Dr. L.P. Seavey, U.S. Quarantine Officer, the first official aboard.

On November 1, customs officers discovered in the pilot house a thin cedar board upon which Tokizo Miki, dying skipper of the ill-fated craft, had scrawled a meager record of events leading to the tragic end.

Translated by H. Kawamura, Japanese consul at Seattle, the rude log listed the names of the twelve crew members and pathetically stated: "We, the above named twelve persons, departed from Misaki, Kanawaga Prefecture, on December 5, fifteenth year of Taisho (1926).

"While at work fishing, a part of the engine was broken. Eight bushels of rice which we had on board has been exhausted. No ships have passed by us. All hope is gone and only death is to be awaited."

The officers also found nine envelopes in which Captain Miki had carefully placed a lock of each man's hair to be returned home for burial in the Buddhist temple, in accordance with Japanese custom. Locks of hair of two of the crewmen who had died the same day were in the same envelope.

On November 2, the craft was towed to Pier 41, Seattle, and it was there on November 4 that customs officers made the dramatic discovery of a diary describing events from the time the vessel set sail from Japan.

It was kept by Sutejiro Izwa until he died March 17, at which time it was taken over by Gennosuke Matsumoto, who was the last to die and whose body was found huddled alongside that of the captain. It is a revealing insight into the thoughts of men who faced inevitable death.

Translated by Consul Kawamura, it reads in part:

December 5, 1926, zero a.m. From Misaki harbor, we sailed on off Choji, on our eighth sailing.

December 9. Fishing with good result—taking two hundred pounds red fish and four sharks and four other fine fish.

December 12. Ship's crank shaft broke early this day and we are helpless. We tried to hoist sails. But on account of strong west winds we could not sail as we desired. The ship drifted on out of control.

December 14. Snow is beginning to fall without wind. We decided we must use rice sparingly. While we were eating breakfast, we sighted in northern direction a ship of about twenty tons. We signaled them by raising our flag, but they were out of sight.

December 16. At 7 a.m. we sighted a T.K.K. steamer and thought at last the favor of God was upon us. We raised two flags and kindled fire on deck and made a great noise. But the steamer proceeded off our track.

We sighted a fishing boat at 10 a.m. in a southwesterly direction and we signaled in various ways in vain, as it was out of sight in thirty minutes.

West wind began to blow. We were drifting helplessly.

December 18. For eighteen hours this day we sailed west. We rested at 4 p.m. and had conference. There was no hope of meeting a steamboat and we decided to head for Bonin Island (about five hundred miles southeast of Yokohama) and try our luck in meeting a steamer then, but it would take three or four months to reach it.

December 19. West winds all morning. Waves running high and we drifted on west wind for thirty hours. We are headed for Bonin Island and we think how long it takes it to wash us there. If we are out of luck, our fate is ended.

December 20. A jewel north wind is blowing and everything O.K. When the westerly winds were blowing day after day the captain began to talk of taking big chance and heading for America. The crew objected to that plan.

December 21. We were helpless and drifting before the wind going west. We all worshipped Konpira [Japanese god of seafaring men] at the shrine. We drew lots which indicated west and so we headed west.

December 23. Boat still drifting. At 5 p.m. we caught a 160-pound fish. We almost despaired of sailing west, yet in going toward the east it would take four months to reach America. It is too late to hope to meet a boat, and it is not manly to wait.

December 26. Unable to head west, we have at last turned toward the east. We have finally decided to risk all and head for America.

December 28. Drifting westward with heavy wind shoving at the stern. If this keeps up ten days we may be carried to land. This day we caught bonita. We dried the fish to preserve them. The rice is giving out.

It is after midnight. As the captain is without definite course, his heart is filled with trouble. We dare not express to each other our innermost thoughts.

We prayed to Konpira and promised him that we would never again ask of him unreasonable. Even our deepest prayers do not draw pity from our angry god! Oh, Konpira! Have pity on us or we shall throw away thy charms. No—No—No—No—oh, let us not think such heresy!

Konpira is still there. He is for right and justice. The

evil that we think is in our minds. Have mercy on us, oh, Konpira. We heed your warning and suffer in all humility. Please pity and forgive us!

December 31. We are drifting again. This is the last of the year. Greetings and a happy new year to everybody! Pray God to help us.

January 1 [1927]. New Year Day, the sixteenth year of Taisho [the era fixed by the reigning Japanese emperor]. We celebrated this day by mixing rice and red beans and enjoying the luxury of koya jofu [dried bean cakes]. We confessed to each other many of our innermost thoughts—and then came night. At 7 p.m. we are again becalmed and drifting.

January 3. We have had three good days of weather and our spirits have been high as we celebrated New Year Day for three consecutive days. But fear is in our hearts again—whither are we bound? The sea is all about us and we have no compass to guide.

January 4. Praise be to Konpira! He has sent us rain. We gathered it in canvases and shall hoard it as a miser hoards his gold.

January 7. We are still groping our way about the sea. We have tried to set our course by the sun, but all is in vain. We drift, drift in an endless sea.

January 17. [Here the diarist stated tersely:] We have repaired our engine. [Obviously he was suffering hallucinations, for no previous reference to repairs had been made, and the very next day he confided to his diary:] We are still drifting.

January 27. A ship! A ship! Happy madness seizes us as we sight a steamer. We build a fire—we wave, we shout, we dance—but, oh, Konpira! The stranger does not see us and is gone over the horizon. Alas, again we are drifting we know not whither. The sea is mighty. Oh, Konpira, are you without mercy?

February 1. We caught one fish and ate it for dinner.

February 13. Sickness is upon us. Hatuzo Terada has lain in his bunk past five days and is wasting away. We have caught more fish to eat. Yukichi Tsume Mitsu has hurt his leg and has taken to his bunk. Who shall be next?

March 5. Today at breakfast we had no food. [On the next day Captain Miki wrote the cedar-board message of despair.]

March 9. Denjiro Hosai this day died of illness. Tsumetaro Naoye now sick. Big bird was caught. [It was later determined that the birds were caught on tuna hooks baited with human flesh.]

March 17. There being no wind, we repaired the sails. Sutejiro Izawa died. [Izawa had kept the diary up till this time. Matsumoto continued it until his death.]

March 22. There appeared a seal. We thought we were not far from shore. Tsupiuchi became ill from several days ago.

March 27. Clouds and a southwest wind. As it was an adverse wind we drifted. Terada and Yokota died today. We caught a large bird.

March 29. Rain. North-northwest wind changed to south-southwest wind at 3 p.m. We are drifting average of four miles an hour on account of the strong wind. Tokichi Kuwata died at 9 a.m. and Tokakichi Mitani died during the night. We caught a shark.

[Now the diary shortens. Drifting, illness and death are the most common entries.]

April 6. Tsunjiuchi died . . . April 14. Yukichi Tsunemitsu died . . . April 19. Yoshishiro Udehira died . . .

April 27. We have drifted 140 days now. Our strength is gone. We are waiting for our time to come.

May 5. From morning to 6 p.m. it was clear. And I being ill, I could not longer stand at the wheel, but I had to guide the ship. I cannot lose my life.

May 6. Captain Tokizo Miki became very ill.

May 10. No clouds. Northwest wind. Hard wind and high waves. Ship adrift with rolled up sails. Ship speeding forward south-southwest. I am suffering of the captain's complaints. Illness.

This is the last entry written by the dying Matsumoto, For nearly six months more the luckless craft was destined to drift unseen until sighted by the *Margaret Dollar's* lookout.

On November 3, Captain Robert Dollar, president of the Dollar Steamship Company, telegraphed Consul Kawamura, expressing sorrow at the calamity, disclaiming all salvage rights, and offering to return the craft to the owners in Japan on the deck of the S.S. *President Madison*, with the recommendation that proceeds from the sale of the vessel go to the families of the dead fishermen.

The families telegraphed a reply declining the offer; for, they said, the evil spirits aboard the bewitched ship would cause an exodus of the inhabitants from the village where she was owned.

She was cursed by Konpira from the moment she was launched in the spring of 1926, they lamented, for she was the first ship of her kind to flaunt tradition, being the first "great ship," five times the size of the vessels that had been used by Japanese in that area throughout the centuries.

To offset the wrath of Konpira, they said, on her maiden voyage her crew sailed her 250 miles down the coast to Konpira's shrine, where the ancient ritual of dedicating the vessel to the god was scrupulously observed.

It was to no avail.

On November 3, the two withered bodies were cremated, and on November 7, black-robed Chyoaui Ike, Buddhist priest, chanted last rites before an improvised, incense-burning altar in a Seattle mortuary. On the altar were the weathered cedar board with its scrawled message of lost hope, an urn containing the ashes of the two bodies, and nine small envelopes with the locks of hair.

The death ship's doomed career ended December 19 when she was towed to Richmond Beach, on Puget Sound north of Seattle, soaked with oil and burned—intact.

Morbid irony is revealed in the translation of the vessel's name. Ryo Yei Maru means Good and Prosperous.

20. Pacific Paroxysm

Women, like storms at sea, often precede angry upsurgings with deceptive calm that lures men and mariners to disaster. Calm seas rode into mid-October on gentle, variable winds that blessed the land and sea with warm "Indian summer" weather.

Ruth hopped aboard *Tradewinds* on a sunny, windless mid-October morning while I was squatting on the afterdeck readying gear for the day's charter, which I had informed her would be my last before running *Tradewinds* up the coast to the Columbia River for the upriver haul to the Portland marina where I'd arranged for winter moorage.

Without a word she kneeled on deck facing me, pressed her pretty, tanned face bow-on to my sea-weathered one in a nose-rubbing Eskimo smooch, then leaned back and for some seconds locked her gorgeous blue eyes on mine.

"Skipper," she oozed, batting her long blond lashes under seductively lowered lids, "I want you to take me on the cruise to Portland."

"Oh, no!" I boomeranged. "A trip like that is too risky and tough for little girls."

Without changing expression, she twined her fingers around my neck, hauled me close and kissed me—hard.

"Please, skipper," she purred during the come-up-for-air interval, "with brass polish and spar varnish on it."

"NO!" I blurted. "Capital N, capital O—period!" Her feminine pride was breached—but good!

With a blast of air from outthrust lower lip, she blew a stray blond lock from her forehead, exploded to her feet, vaulted to the recently repaired dock and stormed topside up the steps, her shining golden hair bouncing against her haughtily erect shoulders like wind-lashed hemp.

Gaping dumbfounded at her retreating afterside, I could not help admiring the fascinating wiggle in her sternsheets. Before I could reassemble my babe-boggled brain, my charter group arrived and we ka-chucked out the channel onto a mercifully serene sea.

Seething at the sting of Ruth's angry shove-off, I stood sphinx-like at the wheel, glowering at the velvety calm sea's surface as we churned westward.

"The ocean is mighty unpredictable. It can do strange things." The abrupt statement came from a man standing behind me in the wheelhouse.

"Clint Trevor's the name," he said, half shouting to top the clamor of the Frisco Standard. "I'm one of your flat-lander anglers."

His sudden chatter jarred me out of my bitter thoughts. He was one of six fishing passengers aboard, and his friendliness soon dissipated the first impression of sour old age hinted by his iron-gray hair, wrinkled countenance and slightly stooped shoulders.

Gazing at the Pacific's calm, blue-green surface, he told me a terrifying tale of near disaster at sea.

The hair-raising incident happened, he related, during the first World War while he was an army enlisted man standing mid-to-four lookout duty on a dark night on the fantail of one of the United States Army's biggest transports steaming over the mid-Pacific's glassy, windless surface, en route from the United States to the Philippines.

"The ocean was calmer than this"—he swept his arm toward the smooth expanse around us—"when all a sudden for no discernible reason that big ship began heeling to starboard," he recounted. "She kept listing farther and farther until the water was gushing over the starboard bulwark and sluicing across the down-side deck.

"Being dead-center in the stern with my arms locked around the taffrail stanchions, I had a view forward of most of the ship, and I can tell you there was no doubt in my mind that she was going right on over to a capsized plunge to the bottom.

"Loose gear throughout the ship—deck equipment, galley utensils, tools, crates and what not—went crashing to the down side, the whole hellishin' uproar pierced by the yells of sliding, tumbling men clawing for their lives at anything they could grab.

"Seemed like she skidded along nearly on beam-ends forever, the prop thrashing and thumping under her angled counter beneath me.

"After one helluva time she began inching her way upright, then laid sickeningly over the other way in a near capsize to port. After a series of lessening rolls both ways, she steadied to an even keel, and the shook-up bridge crew and engine-room gang got her hove to.

"A quick crew muster revealed cuts, scrapes, bruises and broken bones but miraculously nobody over the side.

"Because of the middle-of-the-night darkness, we couldn't see what caused our near disaster, and our urgent wireless inquiries revealed no unusual disturbances reported by ships, islands or anyone else in the area. It remained an eternal mystery.

"Yep, the ocean can do strange things."

Shouts from the afterdeck cut our conversation short, and we followed the anglers' excited gesticulations to a several-acre area of feeding birds and slowed to rig out and troll.

Twelve salmon and six happy anglers later, we rollicked back to Depoe Bay, where my passengers wished me smooth sailing on my planned voyage to Portland later that week and then took off.

My expectation that Ruth would be on the dock throwing herself at me in weeping remorse for the earlier abruptness revealed my ignorance of the workings of the female mind.

No Ruth.

She must not have been aware that I'd returned to port, I rationalized, and hotfooted to her cottage.

No Ruth. No message. No promise of re-splicing our beautiful relationship. No mere skiff of a girl with golden hair, laughing blue eyes and a heart full of love was about to rattle my keelson.

Spurned I was—yes—but I was also spurred by a lusty

thirst for ocean-wave knowledge uncorked by Clint's tale of the transport's mysterious near capsize.

For starters I hotrodded to the Toledo library and embarked on what has proved to be a huge quest on an immense subject, which through my sea years has steered me into many channels of first-hand ocean observation and research and churned up some toweringly astonishing information . . . .

21. Tsunami

The most devastating, death-dealing natural phenomena known to man are the awesome ocean giants born in violent convulsions beneath the sea's surface.

Commonly known as tidal waves, they are more accurately termed seismic sea waves by oceanographers. In recent years they have been universally labeled tsunami, meaning "harbor wave" in Japanese. Use of the term sprang from the countless tsunamis—more than in any other nation—that have pounded Japanese ports into shambles of death and destruction.

On Monday, June 26, 1896, one of Japan's most disastrous tsunamis decimated the Sanriku District on the northeast coast of Honshu, three hundred miles north of Tokyo, where thousands of Japanese had gathered to celebrate Sanno-Sai, one of the nation's three great Shinto festivals.

At 7:32 p.m. a violent seaquake wrenched the ocean floor in Tuscarora Deep, 120 miles to the east. Only a slight tremor was felt on the Sanriku coast, and the celebrants, accustomed to earth paroxysms in the quake-prone area, continued their revelry.

Twenty minutes later the sea began silently receding from the Sanriku shore, creeping outward beyond the limits of the lowest tides, exposing seafloor never before seen within the memory of man. The ominous absence of the normal sounds of the surf was nature's warning of impending doom, but the celebrants ignored it and continued celebrating into the gathering dusk.

After a few moments of uncanny silence, a whispering

from the shoreline grew to a rattling sound, as from pebbles rolling on a wave washed beach; then rapidly the whispering swelled to a thundering roar as a monstrous breaker towering an estimated 110 feet above the revelers' heads slammed millions of tons of rampaging water inshore.

The behemoth engulfed hundreds of miles of coastline, obliterating scores of villages with their entire populaces and ravaging the countryside for hundreds of yards inland. A shockingly difficult post-mortem revealed 27,122 lives lost, thousands injured and homeless, and over 10,600 homes destroyed.

Tragic instances of the terrible force of monster seas— some chronicled, some the theorized cause of ancient disasters—stretch back to antiquity.

A giant tsunami, whipped up in the Arabian Sea in 1945, inspired investigating scientists to speculate that a similiar huge sea wave may have caused the Biblical flood of Noah's ark fame that inundated the Tigris and Euphrates River valleys for 150 days, five thousands years ago.

The greatest cataclysm in recorded history occurred between 1500 and 1400 B.C. when a titanic volcanic explosion on Thera Island in the Aegean Sea pulverized fifteen cubic miles of solid rock and sent tidal waves of staggering height hurtling onto shores all around the Mediterranean, obliterating the powerful Minoan civilization.

Scientists have discovered remarkable similarities between Plato's discoveries about the legendary lost continent of Atlantis and the decimation of Thera, which scientists feel could well have been Atlantis before it disappeared beneath the sea.

Ancient Greek historians tell of the total destruction of the town of Helice and its entire population beneath the waters of the Gulf of Corinth in the third century B.C.; and ancient records describe great waves that rose along the eastern shores of the Mediterranean in A.D. 358, sweeping completely over islands and low-lying shores, leaving boats on the housetops of Alexandria and drowning thousands of people.

On June 7, 1692, immense earthquake-spawned seas swept over Port Royal, Jamaica, destroying the town and killing thousands of inhabitants. Force and size of the killer seas are dramatically pointed up by the terrifying recorded experience of the big English frigate HMS *Swan*.

Caught in the Port Royal careening slip, the *Swan* was swept completely over the town. People struggling in the water above housetops clutched for their lives at her trailing rigging as she was catapulted before the onslaught and was finally dumped into the sea on the other side of the town, where she soon sank.

The saints must have been chagrined when in Lisbon, Portugal, on All Saints Day in 1755, a massive earthquake churned up giant seas that dealt wholesale death and destruction along the coasts of Portugal, Spain, Tangier and Morocco; then swept to the English Channel and raced completely across the Atlantic in nine and a half hours, raising the sea level twelve feet above normal at Barbados in the West Indies.

Old records reveal that in 1868, shortly after nearly three thousand miles of the western coast of South America was convulsed by earthquakes, the sea receded from shore, leaving ships that had been at anchor in forty feet of water stranded on harbor bottoms until a gargantuan wave came roaring inshore, rampaging through towns and hurling vessels up to a mile inland.

One victim was the two-hundred-foot iron sidewheeler gunboat USS *Wateree*, which was swept from its anchorage at Arica, Peru, bowled completely over the town, and dumped upright and intact among sand dunes a mile inland, never to return to the sea.

In August, 1883, the greatest known volcanic explosion, since Thera, pulverized the island of Krakatoa in the Sunda Strait between Java and Sumatra and generated the worst tsunami catastrophe in modern history. Incredibly, the actual sounds of the series of explosions were heard as far as Rodriguez Island in the Indian Ocean, three thousand miles distant.

The colossal upheaval lashed hundred-foot sea waves into hurtling walls of destruction that demolished entire towns, killed more than 36,000 people, traveled 7,800 miles to Cape Horn, and were felt in the English Channel, 11,040 miles away.

Modern times have brought no respite from giant killer waves. On April Fools' Day in 1946, nature played a tragic tsunami trick. In the pre-dawn darkness on that bleak April first off barren Unimak Island—first and largest in Alaska's nine-hundred-mile Aleutian Chain—the earth's guts shook in a mighty convulsion that collapsed a mammoth segment of the steep, submerged Aleutian Trench wall, sending a multi-million-ton rock avalanche roaring to the sea floor nearly eighteen thousand feet below.

The stupendous upheaval lashed hundred-foot swells into a rushing sweep across the North Pacific. An early victim was the "impregnable" reinforced-concrete Scotch Cap Lighthouse which towered ninety-two feet above the sea on Unimak Island, where it guarded the heavily traveled sea passage connecting the North Pacific Ocean with the Bering Sea.

The first roaring juggernaut engulfed the entire Scotch Cap headland and lighthouse, leaving only shattered rubble and no sign of the five coastguardsmen who had been manning the lighthouse.

Less than five hours later, the sea began receding from the shores of the Hawaiian Islands, twenty-three hundred miles distant, exposing reefs, harbor bottoms and ocean floor more than five hundred feet beyond the normal low-tide line.

The series of churning inrushes which followed swept scores of homes, buildings and people to oblivion. Moving at a speed of 470 miles an hour, the giant waves measured ninety miles between crests and were recorded eighteen hours after their violent Aleutian birth as far south as Valparaiso, Chile, more than eight thousand miles from the epicenter.

The sea gods seem to have a morbid penchant for throwing their hardest punches on man's special days. In Alaska, on Good Friday, March 27, 1964, Mother Earth shook her bowels in a violent spasm that stands as one of the strongest earthquakes ever recorded on the North American Continent.

The Great Alaskan Earthquake and the rampaging monster sea waves it created killed 181 people and caused more than $750 million in damage.

Highest point affected by the behemoth first wave was 220 feet above sea level near Valdez, Alaska, where it ripped out a land mass four thousand feet long and six hundred feet wide, establishing itself as the highest true tsunami ever recorded.

After devastating widespread Alaskan coastal areas, the giant wave roaring south at a computed 430 miles an hour wiped out fifteen lives and wreaked millions of dollars in damage along the west coast of the United States mainland.

Depoe Bay escaped with minimal damage because it caught the lateral or side effect. As the crests of the immense seas surged past on a north-to-south heading, water came cascading through the gorge-like channel like a mountain cataract for up to forty-five minutes without cessation, flooding the harbor and surrounding area many feet above normal high-tide limits.

Then after a few moments of eerie quiet, the water went brawling out the channel to the ocean as the troughs surged past, draining the bay nearly dry. This oscillation continued in gradually lessening degrees for over ninety-six hours.

At Beverly Beach State Park, five miles south of Depoe Bay, it surged inshore and engulfed a family camping far above reach of highest known tide, snatching four children to their deaths.

Two hundred and fifty miles to the south it roared into the harbor at Crescent City, California, demolishing most waterfront installations and killing eleven people.

Hurtling on like unleashed giants, the killer waves rampaged across the entire length of the Pacific and were recorded in the Antarctic Ocean twenty-two and a half hours after their raging birth in Alaska.

Shock waves oscillated the water as far away as Key West, Florida, and created surges along the Gulf coast of Louisiana and Texas that broke vessels from their moorings at New Orleans when the Mississippi River suddenly rose a foot and half and ripped three ten-thousand-ton ships from their moorings at Houston, Texas.

Ships at sea are usually unaware of the powerful giants they are steaming over, for according to marine scientists, the main force of these juggernauts drives through the sea beneath the surface at up to 550 miles per hour, while on

Giant seas spawned in disturbances in the far reaches of the Pacific engulf the rocky shore near Depoe Bay. (Photo by author)

Fishing vessel is hurled onto jagged rocks at south side of Depoe Bay channel entrance. Two crewmen escaped but vessel was a total loss. (From author's collection)

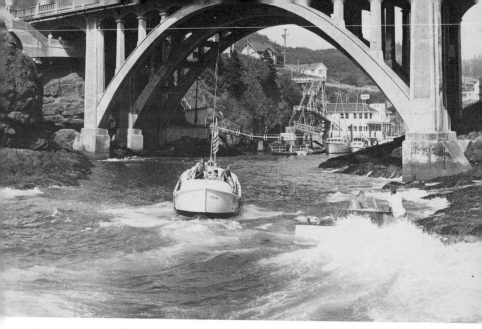

Coast Guard motor lifeboat maneuvers to get tow line to breaker-bashed cabin cruiser on rocks at south side of Depoe Bay channel entrance. (Coast Highway 101 bridge and Depoe Bay harbor in background) (Photo by author)

Small cruiser is slammed high onto rocks just inside Depoe Bay channel entrance. (Photo by author)

Cresting sea hurls troller toward rock-bound Depoe Bay channel entrance. (Photo by author)

Good-Friday, Alaska-spawned tidal wave in 1964 sank fishing vessel *Dolores* in Depoe Bay.
(Photo by author)

the surface their immense reach of up to 150 miles between crests is scarcely perceptible.

When the titanic seas reach shallow water, their lower portions are slowed by frictional drag on the ocean floor, causing them to slow and pile up to staggering heights of a hundred feet or more above the surface, and they come raging into shorelines and ocean-edge installations with shattering force.

Marine scientists have determined that a tsunami moving through water twenty thousand feet deep will hurtle along at about 545 miles an hour, and have calculated that a mere twenty-foot wave surging ashore at forty-five miles per hour has a crushing force of about two tons per square foot.

The biggest known waves were not bona fide tsunamis but the result of massive rock avalanches hurtling down precipitous, exposed slopes into bodies of water at their bases. Such an avalanche churned the most monstrous wave in recorded history into roaring action at Lituya Bay on the Alaskan Panhandle, 115 miles northwest of Juneau.

On July 9, 1958, an earthquake sent an estimated ninety million tons of rock thundering down a three-thousand-foot-high slope into Gilbert Inlet at the head of the bay.

The cataclysmic impact blasted a monster wave into a leaping hundred-miles-per-hour sweep across the inlet, where it roared over the 1,740-foot summit of the steep slope, forming the opposite shore and rampaged nearly three-fourths of a mile inland, destroying four square miles of heavy forest.

Probable solution of Clint Trevor's tale of the army transport's mysterious near-capsize flashed into focus with the account of a similar harrowing occurrence decades later. The night of December 9, 1970, the palatial cruise liner *Bergensfjord* was steaming northward on a calm sea in six hundred fathoms along the Pacific coast of South America.

Shortly before midnight the passengers were jarred awake by the sudden frenetic shaking of the ship, followed by an abrupt listing as though it had run onto a ponderous submerged object. The ship finally righted itself and was hove to while all hands and passengers donned life jackets and reported to their boat stations.

A thorough inspection revealed no damage, and the ship, abuzz with speculation as to the cause of the mysterious paroxysm, proceeded on course.

The following day a radio news broadcast told of a violent earthquake that had occurred off the coast of Peru the previous night. Its epicenter proved to be only seventy miles from the ship's position at that time. Shock waves from the ocean-floor quake were the obvious cause of the ship's strange convulsions, and undoubtedly provided the solution to scores of previous unsolved sea mysteries.

22. Giants of the Wind

Tsunamis are hatched suddenly in evil turmoil in the earth's guts and often pounce on their victims with little or no warning.

Wind waves, though more frequent and often lethal, are usually born slowly and precede their onslaughts with warnings such as falling barometers, muggy atmosphere, long mare's tail cirrus clouds, and misty halos around the sun and moon, affording mariners a fighting chance to prepare and pit skill, judgment and seamanship against their wind-sea adversaries.

Potential giant wind waves usually first appear as tiny wind-gusted cat's paws chasing each other across the sea's surface. When gusts settle to a steady two-to-three miles per hour, tiny ripples begin to cavort along the surface. A four-mile-per-hour wind builds them to baby waves with enough height to give the wind pushing surface.

As wind velocity increases the waves gain height, and the wind gets an even better crack at their windward slopes, shoving them ever higher and faster. A sailor's rule of thumb is that a wave will be half as high as the speed of the driving wind.

The size that the growing waves attain depends not only on the wind velocity but also on the "fetch"—the distance the waves are driven by the wind. The longer the fetch, the higher the waves. In restricted waterways with short fetch, waves reach heights of about twelve feet, but in open expanses they can rear to over hundred-foot crests.

The highest wind wave ever recorded by a ship at sea was a 112-foot colossus logged by the 478-foot naval tanker USS

On-board photo of bow of merchant ship about to slam into towering, wind-driven sea. (From author's collection)

Tanker buries bow in hurtling wind-generated sea. (From author's collection)

Ramapo while running before sixty-knot winds between Manila and San Diego in February, 1933.

The wind had been blowing from astern unabated for seven days with a fetch of thousands of miles of open Pacific, generating a wave speed of over fifty knots. The watch officer, noticing the approach of an immense series of following seas, logged them at a consecutive 80, 90, 100, and 107 feet; then recorded the fantastic 112-foot giant.

Running in the same direction as the seas, the tanker handled them with no strain, but accounts of ships crashing to disaster while butting into heavy seas are legion throughout maritime history.

"Holes in the sea"—sudden canyon-like troughs followed by towering crests—have trapped many ships. Particularly "hole prone" are the sea lanes off the southeast coast of Africa, where the powerful southwest—surging Alguhas Current collides head-on with heavy storm-driven swells churning in from the southwest.

During World War II the British cruiser HMS *Birmingham*, steaming off the coast of South Africa between Durban and Cape Town, abruptly plummeted into a hole in the sea. Before she could recover, a monster sea came rampaging over the bow, engulfing A and B turrents in solid water that swept over the open bridge, sixty feet above the waterline.

In August, 1964, the 750-foot *Edinburgh Castle*, steaming without difficulty into heavy southwesterly swells in the same vicinity, suddenly plunged bow-on into a hole in the sea at a thirty-degree angle. Before the bow could rise, the next sea steam-rollered aboard in a solid, towering wave, smashing deck gear and hurling rails, ladders and gear over the side.

Slamming into heavy gale-driven seas at reduced speed off Durban on May 17, 1974, the 132,000-ton, fully-loaded Norwegian tanker *Wilstar* nearly sank when she smashed into a hole in the sea, then was mauled by a monstrous wave that completely submerged the main deck and tore off her huge, bulbous bow, shearing off steel plates nearly an inch thick and snapping heavy steel beams like laths.

The *Wilstar*, like the *Birmingham* and *Edinburgh Castle*, licked its wounds and was able to limp to port, but marine annals are pocked with accounts of victims torn apart and sunk.

A tragic South African sea-lanes casualty was the twenty-eight-thousand-ton tanker *World Glory*. Steaming sixty-five miles off Durban in 1968, it smashed into a giant sea that wrenched it in two and sent it plummeting to the bottom.

Davy Jones's morbid disaster log reaches throughout all the earth's seas. The ocean giants play no favorites. The largest liners afloat are not invulnerable. In the late winter of 1942, the thousand-foot, eighty-one-thousand-ton Cunard liner *Queen Mary* came within inches of capsizing seven hundred miles west of the English coast.

Fighting eastward through a vicious storm with fifteen thousand American troops aboard, the great liner was slammed broadside by a mammoth wave that heeled her so far to port her upper decks were awash. Veteran crewmen were certain she was doomed to history's worst wave-capsize catastrophe, and declared that the few inches constituting another five degrees roll would have finished her.

In April, 1966, the Italian Line's forty-four-thousand-ton luxury liner *Michelangelo* was thrashing through a raging Atlantic storm eight hundred miles off New York City when it was struck by a monstrous wave that inumdated the entire forward half of the ship, crumpling the flare of its bow, ripping off forty feet of railing and bulwark, smashing a hole in the curved superstructure, and breaking heavy glass eighty feet above the waterline.

Tons of water stove in sturdy bulkheads seventy feet above the roiling sea's surface and rampaged into the ship's interior. Two passengers and a crewman were killed, and scores were injured. The giant seas' death log sweeps on.

In March, 1971, the 632-foot tanker *Texas Oklahoma*, loaded to her Plimsolls with fuel oil, was slugging up the Atlantic coast from Port Arthur, Texas, to Boston when rising winds off Florida forced her to reduce speed. She was soon slamming into sixty-knot northeasterly winds and forty-foot waves. The strain was too much.

Several hours' bludgeoning tore her in two amidships. The bow section sank with all thirteen crewmen caught there, and the wallowing stern was hammered to the depths twenty-seven hours later. All the officers were lost, and of her total complement of forty-four men, only thirteen survived.

In 1976, four hundred miles southwest of Bombay, India, the Cypriot tanker *Cretan Star* flashed a radio message that she had been hit by a huge wave; then vanished with all hands, leaving only an oil slick and scattered flotsam.

A monster wave was the suspect cause of the disappearance with all aboard of the eighteen-thousand-ton Panamanian tanker *Grand Zenith* thirty miles east of Cape Sable, Nova Scotia, in December, 1976.

The demons' broth churned up in the area curving from southeast to southwest off the Aleutians on the Great Circle shipping route between the Pacific Northwest and the Orient has dashed staggering numbers of ships and mariners to oblivion. This North Pacific cauldron churns and boils almost incessantly during the fall and winter months and sometimes catches mariners unawares during spring and summer storms.

The ingredients for violence plague the area. Strong currents and tides, and cold sea and air masses from the Arctic—in collision with warm water and air borne from the southern reaches of the Pacific—churn the sea into frenzy in a nightmare of fierce, shrieking winds and paralyzing cold. Through the years, the area has taken a terrible toll of ships and men.

On January 9, 1952, Captain George Plover of the American merchant ship *Pennsylvania*, pounding toward the Orient eight hundred miles northwest of the Columbia River, radioed that heavy seas had carried away deck cargo, torn off hatch covers and split a fourteen-foot crack in the hull, necessitating abandon-ship preparations. No further word was heard. A Coast Guard air-sea search turned up floating debris, a capsized lifeboat and no survivors.

The twelve-thousand-ton Liberian-registered merchant ship *Pacrover* radioed on December 24, 1972, that she was sinking in fifty-five-foot seas off the Aleutians and abandoning ship. Searchers found four overturned lifeboats and fragmented wreckage floating in an oil slick, but no survivors.

Twenty-seven life-jacketed bodies but no survivors were recovered of the crew of forty that were aboard the fifteen-thousand-ton Liberian freighter *Oriental Monarch* after it was hammered to the bottom in heavy seas five hundred miles northwest of Vancouver Island, British Columbia, while steaming from Portland, Oregon, to Japan with a cargo of grain in December, 1973.

All twenty-eight hands were lost when the eleven-thousand-ton lumber-laden Hong Kong freighter *Geranium*, bound from Port Angeles, Washington, to Osaka, Japan, sank in a storm south of the Aleutians in November, 1974.

The doomsday log lashes on.

The twenty-one-thousand-ton, steel-laden Philippine freighter *Transocean Shipper* disappeared with all thirty-three hands while steaming the Great Circle route from Japan to New Westminster, British Columbia, in February, 1975.

In February, 1977, the Portland-owned, five-hundred-foot merchant ship *Rose S.* vanished with its thirty-one crewmen while heading for Japan with a cargo of logs loaded at Vancouver, British Columbia.

Sixty-four crewmen, four wives of crewmen and two children were lost in the North Pacific cauldron when the Shipping Corporation of India's twenty-one-thousand-ton, wheat-laden bulk carrier *Chandra Gupta* was dashed to eternity while steaming from Portland to Iran in January, 1978.

Friday, the thirteenth of March, 1981, was the tragic jinx date that claimed the lives of all twenty-six crewmen aboard the 105-foot Japanese fishing vessel *Daito Marv 55* when storm waves hammered it to the bottom of the frigid Bering Sea, 380 miles northwest of Adak Island in the Aleutians.

The awesome magnitude of the North Pacific wave potential is startlingly revealed in the findings of a wind and wave investigation made by scientists in the Gulf of Alaska. Based on a study of the worst storms that beset the area over a twenty-year period, the study team concluded that the maximum possible wave could reach an astounding height of 198 feet.

Hurricanes in the Atlantic and typhoons in the Pacific churn up their own murderous brand of wave horror. The predominant hatching area for these massive circular storms is between latitudes fifteen and thirty degrees.

In the northern hemisphere they are usually whipped to violent birth in the Caribbean in the Atlantic, and between the Philippines and Marianas Islands in the western Pacific, from where they go brawling north in raging fifty- to five-hundred-mile-diameter spirals, whirling counter-clockwise. In the southern hemisphere they swirl south with clockwise rotation.

The giant whirlwinds reach hurricane/typhoon status at 74 miles per hour and have been recorded to 186 miles per hour, when wind gauges blew away.

Estimated velocities have topped two hundred miles per hour in the critical pole-side quadrants of their bludgeoning frontal semi-circles, which pack the strongest wallop as they rampage across the sea with fetches of thousands of miles.

Hurricanes and typhoons are like a giant "doughnut" of fierce winds, clouds and heavy rain, with an average fifteen-mile-diameter center called the eye, which is nearly clear and windless, sometimes deceiving mariners into thinking the storm is over. The respite is brief. Shortly, the other side of the hurricane or typhoon roars in with renewed fury.

The worst Atlantic hurricanes usually strike in August through November. Pacific typhoons stretch most of their terror from July through November. Their ferocity is appalling.

The most death-dealing hurricane, among scores that have mauled the United States this century, killed six thousand people when it raged across Galveston Island, Texas, September 8, 1900. The most disastrous typhoon in recorded history walloped the mouth of the Hooghly River on the Bay of Bengal in India, October 7, 1737, destroying over twenty thousand vessels and drowning more than three hundred thousand people.

23. Hell with the Hatches Open

Bright afternoon dwindled to hazy dusk as I forged through wave research in the Toledo library that sultry October day in 1938. A hallucinating stupor half-masted my eyelids and shifted my brain to a dream-wracked trance. Lashing winds transformed to blasts of air from Ruth's outthrust lower lip. Leaping sea crests became her tossing blond head.

I jerked awake, shelved the book I'd been reading, strode outside into a sticky-still evening bathed in gauzy light from a halo-encircled moon, and highballed to Depoe Bay and Ruth's.

Neighbors mumbled something about her driving off with some slick-haired guy with a black moustache. To h--- with her. I'd get a good night's sleep and the next day round up a couple guys to go with me and set sail up the coast for the Columbia River and Portland.

As I blustered through *Tradewind's* wheelhouse on the way to my bunk, I tapped the barometer. It fell a couple of notches. The night was muggy-warm. I flopped on my bunk sans covers and awaited the blessed sleep that would shut out the mental turmoil of wind, waves and women.

Sleep would not come.

Several tossing hours later I lapsed into a sort of nightmare melange of monster seas and slashing winds and weirdly alluring women, like the fabled sirens of ancient times, coaxing me with seductive smiles and song to death in the wild waves. A crashing comber drove me to the depths and smashed me into the forty-fathom bottom, jarring me awake in an arm-flailing sweat.

A pot of strong, hot coffee restored my vision to the spectacle of long cirrus mare's tail clouds streaking across the heavens above the Coast Range in the east, red fire from the rising sun emblazoning the sky's warning of high winds to come. The atmosphere remained ominously quiet and muggy. The barometer crept downward toward the mid-twenty-nine-inch foul-weather sector.

In my experience the two things in this life most radically culpable of numbing a man's brain and atrophying his reasoning power are whiskey and women, with women leading by a liner's length. But no blond babe was gonna leave me in the lurch and gloat at the sight of me grinding my guts in pining ferment.

Nature's sea and weather warnings be damned! I'd set sail for the Columbia at high tide that night.

As I topped *Tradewind's* tanks, stowed chow and gear aboard, and rounded up two naively trusting young land-lubber friends to make the voyage, a hazy halo rode with the sun through the mare's-tail ribbed sky.

Time and tide wait for no man—nor do miffed women!

High tide whispered into Depoe Bay in tomb-like quiet shortly after sunset. My hopes that Ruth would come rushing to the dock at the last minute for a kiss-and-make-up splicing blew to the high, haloed heavens.

My spirits dropped lower than the steadily falling barometer, dragging my normal sense of caution and judgment to the bilge. I vented my frustration on the big flywheel, spun it with malicious vigor, and the Frisco Standard's two big cylinders exploded defiance into the ominous night.

We went thrashing through the channel onto the glowing path laid on the Pacific's deathly calm surface by the mist-veiled moon; then swung north for the Columbia River on what the sea and weather gods were teaming up to make the last voyage on this earth for us mortals who dared defy their warnings.

We chugged smoothly northward till after midnight, failing to heed increasing long swells rolling in from offshore and ignoring the small, dark, cumulus clouds that came scudding in low from the southwest, blotting out the stars and the moon and the high deck of cirrus mare's tails.

Off Cape Kiwanda, twenty-eight miles to the north, tell-tale cat's paws began playing tag across the sea's now-heaving surface in skittering riffles from the southwest, dappled with fitfull rain splatters.

The first screeching blast slammed us from astern as we approached Cape Lookout, thirty-seven miles north of Depoe Bay. The wind subsided briefly, then walloped us again with battering force that mounted to a continuous hammering southwest gale, slamming blinding spray and rain before it in horizontal sheets.

That was when smoke began curling up from under the engine cover, and the Frisco Standard went crazy in raucous pounding.

I shut it off, yanked off the engine cover, and gaped stupefied at the smoking, broken metal pawl that was supposed to engage the clutch and hold it in gear. Friction had worn it red hot and broken it.

In my haste to clear out of Depoe Bay I'd neglected to get the sails from the shed behind Ruth's, where I'd stored them during the fishing season. We were dead in the rampaging water.

The screaming sou'wester heaved us broadside to the mauling waves and began pummeling us toward the towering, sheer black-rock bluffs marking the seaward face of Cape Lookout. Great drunken waves slammed against the cliffs in a spray-shot welter.

I yanked a hunk of rusty metal strap, some wire and pliers from the tool locker, bound the metal hunk to the broken pawl with wire—like splinting a broken bone—seized the wire taut with the pliers, started the Frisco Standard, said a fervent prayer and eased the clutch lever ahead.

The jury-rig held.

We clawed offshore on a bruising westerly heading to gain sea room, heaving and plunging into mounting giant swells and rolling viciously in the battering surface chop slamming us broadside on the new heading.

A hard-won five miles or so offshore we resumed our northerly heading, which eased the merciless rolling but slapped a new hazard on us. The little gillnetter raced ahead to near broaching on the slashing crests, forcing us to chop the throttle, then gun it at the right moment on the wave's backside—a nerve-shattering nightmare.

The demented wind whipped off the wave summits and shot slashing spray clouds clear over the masts as we went yawing and careening up the treacherous coast, caught in the raw, brute forces of wind and waves because of my brash, gal-goaded stupidity in sailing in the face of nature's warnings.

A brutalizing eternity later, "lightning" flashes permeating the roiling murk in purplish flareups off our starboard beam, revealed themselves through a brief rift in the scudding clouds as the powerful flashes beamed out by Tillamook Lighthouse, defying the elements as it had since 1881 on a fist of rock a mile off the rugged, cliff-edged coast.

It forewarned us of the twenty-two miles to go to the Columbia River entrance.

Next warning of our brawling approach to the murkobsured Columbia River bar came in the turbulent, late-afternoon gloom with the sudden appearance of several large fishing vessels slogging slow-bell into the fuming wind and seas.

Then the loom of a freighter butting into the maelstrom bugged our eyes out a fathom when its ponderous bow plunged out of sight in a cavernous trough, then burst toward the cloud-wracked sky in a white-water welter that shot over its highest superstructure.

The vessels' laboring course *into* the turbulence, instead of inshore toward the bar and the safety of the river, failed to rap a warning to my brain. We plunged on, stumbled onto a wildly gyrating channel entrance buoy, and swung blindly inshore toward the scud-shrouded bar—and certain death!

The gods of the skies saved us with a freaky miracle. The shrieking wind tore a rift in the clouds overhead, through which slanting sun shafts briefly lit the bar approach ahead.

We were looking at hell with the hatches open. The bar was a devil's cauldron of crashing breakers from jetty to jetty.

I fought the helm to a desperate, southwesterly offshore heading. Ramming slow-bell into the towering seas, our plight was eased by *Tradewind's* very tininess among the giants, for instead of the bow's plunging into a trough and burying before she could rise to the next juggernaut, she rode up and over them like a cork in a cataract.

My crewmen wrestled the helm and throttle while I squared away the anchor gear for dumping. In the lee of the wheelhouse, I flaked down our hundred fathoms of Manila hemp and ten fathoms of chain, shackled to our twenty-five-pound anchor.

As an extra precaution I wrestled from the hold a fifty-pound square hunk of steel I'd carried for ballast and secured it to the upper end of the anchor chain in the hope that it would keep the anchor flat and its flukes gripping. It was to share honors with the clutch splint as the second hunk of rusty metal that probably saved our lives.

I wired all shackle pins so they wouldn't work loose, double-secured the bitter end of the anchor line to the bow bitt, jammed padding in the chock to prevent chafing, made sure the whole shebang was clear for running, and dumped it into the snarling sea.

Shortly we were jerked violently to windward like a lassoed steer by the tautened anchor line at the start of the wildest, most terrifying night of our existence.

Our lives hung on those tenuous strands of braided Manila line holding us to the bottom, for directly downwind a perilous few miles to the northeast the rampaging cauldron of *Peacock* spit gnashed its murderous fangs, just north of the bar, waiting to add us to the bones of hundreds of ships and mariners ground to oblivion in its breaker-bashed sands before and since the U.S. naval brig *Peacock* was hurled to destruction there, July 18, 1841.

Through the raging night the gillnetter pitched and pounded and rolled and stood on its head, then its stern, and yawed in wild sweeps to port and starboard, like a kite in a gale.

The insane chorus, shrieked by the wind through the rigging, accompanied a devil's tattoo of sea and rain water beating against the hull and house.

The anchor held.

The drowned-out galley range was ripped from its moorings and hurled to the cabin deck. The topside galley stack blew over the side, and we jammed a jacket in the hole it

Coastguardsmen examine the little that remains visible of the freighter SS *Iowa* after it was lost with all thirty-four hands on treacherous Peacock Spit, just north of the Columbia River bar, January 12, 1936, two and a half years before the author's vessel narrowly missed being hurled to destruction in the same place in October, 1938. (Courtesy Oregon Historical Society)

left in the overhead. The cabin was a hodge-podge porridge of food, coffee, milk, stove oil, galley gear and what-not churned with splashing bilge water.

The anchor held.

While I wedged myself in the wheelhouse between the engine housing and forward bulkhead, my crewmen spelled each other at clearing and manning the bilge pump, and trying to grab a few winks in the bunks forward, only to be flipped flailing to the deck, like hotcakes on a spatula.

The anchor held.

During the early morning hours a change seeped into the turbulent atmosphere. The keening wind and driving rain and spray eased to a whisper, then slackened and blasted in lessening fits and starts.

Gradually a lightening in the slate-gray overcast spread, enveloping the sea around us in leaden half-light. At last the wind and rain shut off entirely, leaving only huge westerly swells and the dying surface chop.

The barometer hovered at an alarming low 28.7 inches. The tide was approaching slack flood—the only possible time the bar might be crossed before the elements' next barrage.

Several big, heaving and pitching fishing vessels became visible through the gray light, oilskinned figures braced on their foredecks warping in anchor lines on their windlasses, clueing us to get at the job of hand-heaving ours in. *Trade-winds* boasted no windlass.

The blessed Frisco Standard burst into compliance on the first spin, the clutch splint held, and while I eased *Trade-winds* slow ahead my battered crewmen tackled the job of muscling in the anchor line with its fifty-pound hunk, chain and anchor. It was brutal.

We spelled each other between the helm and bruising anchor haul on the lunging foredeck, cursing the very gear that had almost certainly saved our lives. It was as though some monstrous live thing was playing tug-of-war with us.

Several times that damnably perverse line nearly yanked us overboard, and the miracle of the decade was that we escaped crushing or losing fingers on the bow bitt while trying to gain precious turns. A gain of a yard was a major triumph.

Anxious glances toward the now-visible bar smacked our bloodshot eyes with the sight of the churning wakes of an armada of fishing vessels and merchant ships thrashing across the bar during the briefly safe slack flood period.

If we missed slack flood and were caught outside in the next slammer signaled by the low barometer—!

Desperation shot extra strength to our groaning muscles, and we finally bruted the s.o.b. of a fifty-pound weight aboard, followed by the chain and anchor.

The Frisco Standard ka-chucked raucous music as we careened across the bar over awesomely-mountainous seas that seemed to clutch at their escaping victim in a final lunge of curling crests that waited until we were in safe water above the inner ends of the jetties before they exploded their tons of force in crushing breakers.

24. Escape

Relief at escaping to the safety of the river blanked our boggled brains from the thought of putting in at Astoria to phone our families in Portland that we were safe. We chugged on.

Somewhere along our upriver course a considerate watcher on shore spotted us and got word to our families that we were forging homeward.

When we eased to the Portland dock where I'd prearranged winter moorage, our distraught families stood staring trance-like, as though seeing ghosts from the deep—not knowing whether to embrace us, or upbraid us for our sea-stupid recklessness.

Finally my father yanked a crumpled newspaper from under his arm and thrust it before our bloodshot eyes. Banner headlines screamed news of the hurricane-force winds that had devastated shipping off the northern Oregon coast the past thirty-six hours.

Lead paragraphs shouted the tragic account of several large fishing vessels disabled, sunk, and unreported, with an unknown number of crewmen missing and presumed lost.

Family love won out, of course, and they rushed to embrace us. A warm feeling of gratitude for family devotion and being spared by the murderous elements gripped me, but was soon eroded by gnawing despair at the loss of Ruth's love.

My family finally released me, and a figure sprang from the background shadows in a dazzling yellow streak that catapulted into my arms.

Ruth's bear-hug kiss squeezed out the harsh brain and muscle wrack, and my nightmare thoughts of the gales and the crashing seas and the shipwrecks and the deaths did a high-halyard heave to.

-----end-----

The author steers his fifty-foot charter vessel, *Tradewinds Kingfisher*, outbound from Depoe Bay during Depoe Bay's annual Memorial Day Fleet of Flowers ceremony. Designed by the author, *Kingfisher* is skippered by him and serves as his Tradewinds ocean sportfishing fleet's flagship. (Photo by Jan Riedbercer)

photo by Pamela Matter

ABOUT THE AUTHOR

Following his first turbulent year learning ocean fishing off Depoe Bay in 1938, Stan Allyn returned to the tiny port in 1939 to expand his fleet and, except for four years of Atlantic and South Pacific World War II service in the U.S. Coast Guard, has lived there ever since in an ocean-edge home a block south of the Depoe Bay channel entrance, where he wrote this book between charter-fishing trips.

With his son Richard, Captain Stan still owns and operates Tradewinds Ocean Sportfishing and skippers his firm's fifty-foot flagship—*Tradewinds Kingfisher.*